# Mastering MySQL
# for the Web

## Mastering Computer Science
**Series Editor:** Sufyan bin Uzayr

**Mastering MySQL for Web: A Beginner's Guide**
*Mathew Rooney and Madina Karybzhanova*

**Mastering Python for Web: A Beginner's Guide**
*Mathew Rooney and Madina Karybzhanova*

**Mastering Android Studio: A Beginner's Guide**
*Divya Sachdeva and Reza Nafim*

**Mastering Swift: A Beginner's Guide**
*Mathew Rooney and Madina Karybzhanova*

**Mastering C++: A Beginner's Guide**
*Divya Sachdeva and Natalya Ustukpayeva*

**Mastering Git: A Beginner's Guide**
*Sumanna Kaul, Shahryar Raz, and Divya Sachdeva*

For more information about this series, please visit: https://www.routledge.com/Mastering-Computer-Science/book-series/MCS

*The "Mastering Computer Science" series of books are authored by the Zeba Academy team members, led by Sufyan bin Uzayr.*

*Zeba Academy is an EdTech venture that develops courses and content for learners primarily in STEM fields, and offers education consulting to Universities and Institutions worldwide. For more info, please visit https://zeba.academy*

# Mastering MySQL for the Web

## A Beginner's Guide

**Edited by Sufyan bin Uzayr**

**CRC Press**
Taylor & Francis Group
Boca Raton London New York

CRC Press is an imprint of the
Taylor & Francis Group, an **informa** business

First edition published 2022
by CRC Press
6000 Broken Sound Parkway NW, Suite 300, Boca Raton, FL 33487-2742

and by CRC Press
2 Park Square, Milton Park, Abingdon, Oxon, OX14 4RN

*CRC Press is an imprint of Taylor & Francis Group, LLC*

© 2022 Sufyan bin Uzayr

ISBN: 9781032135137 (hbk)
ISBN: 9781032135120 (pbk)
ISBN: 9781003229629 (ebk)

DOI: 10.1201/9781003229629

Typeset in Minion
by KnowledgeWorks Global Ltd.

# Contents

# About the Editor

**Sufyan bin Uzayr** is a writer, coder, and entrepreneur with more than a decade of experience in the industry. He has authored several books in the past, pertaining to a diverse range of topics, ranging from History to Computers/IT.

Sufyan is the Director of Parakozm, a multinational IT company specializing in EdTech solutions. He also runs Zeba Academy, an online learning and teaching vertical with a focus on STEM fields.

Sufyan specializes in a wide variety of technologies, such as JavaScript, Dart, WordPress, Drupal, Linux, and Python. He holds multiple degrees, including ones in Management, IT, Literature, and Political Science.

Sufyan is a digital nomad, dividing his time between four countries. He has lived and taught in universities and educational institutions around the globe. Sufyan takes a keen interest in technology, politics, literature, history, and sports, and in his spare time, he enjoys teaching coding and English to young students.

Learn more at sufyanism.com.

# CHAPTER 1

# Introduction to MySQL

## IN THIS CHAPTER

➤ Introducing basics of MySQL database management systems

➤ Getting an overview of its main features

➤ Reviewing MySQL major benefits as well as limitations

A database is a great invention that acts as a separate application to store multiple collections of data. Each database has one or more distinct application programming interfaces for producing, accessing, operating, searching, and duplication the data it possesses.

These days it is common to use Relational Database Management Systems (RDBMS) to hold and manage huge

DOI: 10.1201/9781003229629-1

volumes of data. An RDBMS is a software that lets you implement a database with tables, columns, and indexes. It not only guarantees the Referential Integrity between the lines of various tables but also has the capacity to update the indexes automatically. It can also interpret any Structured Query Language (SQL) and combine information from various resources.

To be fair, other kinds of data stores can also be of use, such as files on the file system or large hash tables in memory, but data collecting and writing would not be so fast and simple with that kind of system.

MySQL is one of the open-source RDBMS. It was created by a Swedish company, MySQL AB, founded by Swedes David Axmark, Allan Larsson, and Finland Swede Michael Widenius. Widenius and Axmark began the original development of MySQL in 1994. The first version of MySQL was presented on May 23, 1995. Initially, it was created strictly for personal usage from mini SQL (mSQL) based on the low-level language Indexed Sequential Access Method, which the creators thought to be too slow and at times rigid. Since 1994, five major upgraded version releases took place:[1]

| Release | General Availability | Latest Minor Version | Latest Release | End of Support |
|---------|---------------------|---------------------|----------------|----------------|
| 5.1 | November 14, 2008; 12 years ago | 5.1.73 | 12-03-2013 | Dec 2013 |
| 5.5 | December 3, 2010; 10 years ago | 5.5.62 | 10-22-2018 | Dec 2018 |
| 5.6 | February 5, 2013; 8 years ago | 5.6.51 | 01-20-2021 | Feb 2021 |
| 5.7 | October 21, 2015; 5 years ago | 5.7.33 | 01-18-2021 | Oct 2023 |
| 8.0 | April 19, 2018; 3 years ago | 8.0.25 | 05-11-2021 | Apr 2026 |

If you go back to the very basics, you might wonder—why "MySQL?" The idea behind the name is pretty simple. It stands for a combination of "My," the name of co-founder Michael Widenius's daughter, and "SQL," the abbreviation for Structured Query Language.

MySQL is a free and open-source software under the terms of the GNU General Public License and is also obtainable under a variety of proprietary licenses. Originally, MySQL was owned and sponsored by MySQL AB. However, in October 2005, Oracle Corporation has acquired Innobase OY, the Finnish startup company that developed the third-party InnoDB storage engine that

---

[1] https://www.javatpoint.com/mysql-versions, Javatpoint

allowed MySQL to present such functionality with transactions and foreign keys. Not long after the acquisition, an Oracle press release stated that the contracts that make the company's software available to MySQL AB would be due for renewal (meaning extended renegotiation) sometime around 2006. Then, in April 2006 during the MySQL Users Conference, MySQL AB issued a press statement that confirmed that MySQL AB and Innobase OY agreed to a "multiyear" extension of their contract agreement.

The same year, Oracle Corporation acquired Sleepycat Software, makers of the Berkeley DB, a database engine providing the basis for another MySQL storage item. This had little impact, as Berkeley DB was not widely popular, and was dropped (due to lack of installation) in MySQL 5.1 release in October 2006.

Two years after that, in January 2008, Sun Microsystems bought MySQL AB for $1 billion. In April 2009, Oracle Corporation entered into an agreement to purchase Sun Microsystems, together with the MySQL copyright and trademark. Sun's board of directors approved the deal in complete accord. It was also approved by Sun's shareholders and by the US government on August 20, 2009. On December 14, 2009, Oracle stated that it would not stop to further advance MySQL as it had done for the previous 4 years.

Such rapid expansion has resulted in a movement against Oracle's acquisition of MySQL AB, also known as "Save MySQL" from Oracle action that was started by one of the MySQL AB founders, Monty Widenius. Together with his team of IT experts, they collected a petition of 50,000+ developers and users and called upon the European

Commission to veto the approval of the acquisition. At the same time, some Free Software opinion leaders (including the cocounsel of the merger regulation procedure) advocated for the unconditional approval of the merger. As part of the negotiations with the European Commission, Oracle has committed that the MySQL server will operate until at least 2015 and use the dual-licensing strategy long applied by MySQL AB, with proprietary and General Public License versions available. The antitrust of the European Union (EU) had been ready to spare MySQL by refusing the condition for approval but, as revealed by WikiLeaks, the US Department of Justice, at the request of Oracle, supposedly pressured the EU to approve the merger unconditionally. The European Commission, therefore, had no other choice but to unconditionally approve Oracle's acquisition of MySQL AB on January 21, 2010.

In January 2010, before Oracle's acquisition of MySQL AB, Widenius started a General Public License only startup project, MariaDB. MariaDB is a brand positioned to be an alternative to MySQL but is based on the same code base of MySQL server 5.5, aiming to maintain compatibility with other Oracle-provided versions.

A relational database like MySQL organizes data into one or more data tables in which data types are in direct relation to each other; these relations therefore assist to structure the data correctly. SQL is a language programmers apply to create, edit, and extract data from the relational database as well as manage user access to the database. In addition to relational databases and SQL, an RDBMS like MySQL collaborates with an operating system to execute a relational database in a computer's storage system and administer users, allows for network access, and ensures testing database integrity and creation of backups.

In addition to that, MySQL has stand-alone clients that let users interact directly with a MySQL database using SQL, but more often, MySQL is activated in cooperation with other programs to implement applications that require relational database assistance. People also might be familiar with MySQL as a component of the LAMP web application software stack, which is an acronym for Linux, Apache, MySQL, Perl/PHP/Python. Similarly, MySQL is used by many database-driven web applications, including Drupal, Joomla, phpBB, and WordPress. MySQL is also used by many popular websites, including Facebook, Flickr, MediaWiki, Twitter, and YouTube.

MySQL is written in C and C++, but its SQL parser is written in Yacc, meaning it also uses a home-brewed lexical analyzer. Additionally, MySQL works on many system platforms, including AIX, BSDi, FreeBSD, HP-UX, ArcaOS, eComStation, IBM i, IRIX, Linux, macOS, Microsoft Windows, NetBSD, Novell NetWare, OpenBSD, OpenSolaris, OS/2 Warp, QNX, Oracle Solaris, Symbian, SunOS, SCO OpenServer—just to name a few. A port of MySQL to OpenVMS is also available on an open-source basis. Support can be obtained from the official manual, while free support additionally can be accessed through different Internet Relay Chats or forums. Oracle also offers paid support via its MySQL Enterprise products, but they widely differ in the scope of services and in price. On top of that, a number of third-party organizations exist to provide support and services.

## DATABASE BASICS

Before we proceed to explain the insights of MySQL database system in detail, it is necessary to revise a few key definitions related to the database structure:[2]

- **Database:** A database can be described as a collection of tables, with related data.

- **Table:** A table is a matrix with data. A table in a database typically looks like a simple spreadsheet.

---

[2] https://cloudxlab.com/assessment/displayslide/1384/mysql-database-terminology, CloudxLab

- **Column:** One column (data element) contains data of one and the same kind, for example, the column postcode.

- **Row:** A row (= tuple, entry, or record) is a group of related data, for example, the data of one subscription.

- **Redundancy:** Storing data twice, redundantly to make the system faster.

- **Primary Key:** A primary key is unique. A key value cannot occur twice in one table. With a key, you can only find one row.

- **Foreign Key:** A foreign key is a linking pin between two tables.

- **Compound Key:** A compound key (composite key) is a key that consists of multiple columns because one column is not sufficiently unique.

- **Index:** An index in a database resembles an index at the back of a book.

- **Referential Integrity:** Referential Integrity makes sure that a foreign key value always points to an existing row.

## MySQL DATABASE

MySQL is a fast, easy-to-use RDBMS that is utilized by many small and big businesses. MySQL is so widely popular because of many different reasons:

- First of all, it is released under an open-source license. So you do not have to pay anything to use it.

- It is a very powerful program in its own right. It manages a large subset of the functionality of the most complex and powerful database packages.

- MySQL uses a standard form of the well-known SQL data language.

- It can work on many operating systems and in integration with many languages such as PHP, PERL, C, C++, and JAVA.

- MySQL works very quickly and operates well even with truly massive data sets.

- It is not only user-friendly to its developer community but also very friendly to PHP, the most applied language for web development.

- It can support large databases that are up to 50 million rows or more in a table. Normally, the default file size limit for a table is 4GB, but you can increase this (given that your operating system can stretch like this) to a theoretical limit of 8 million terabytes.

- MySQL is very customizable. The open-source public license invites programmers from all over the world to freely modify the MySQL software to fit their own specific needs and desires.

As already mentioned, SQL is the core of a relational database which is great for accessing and administering the database. By using SQL, you can include, update, or remove rows of data, deliver subsets of information, edit databases and perform many other actions. The different subsets of SQL are the following:

- **Data Definition Language (DDL):** It allows you to perform various operations on the database such as CREATE, ALTER, and DELETE objects.

- **Data Manipulation Language (DML):** It allows you to access and manipulate data. It helps you to insert, update, delete, and retrieve data from the database.

- **Data Control Language (DCL):** It allows you to control access to the database. Example—Grant or Revoke access permissions.

- **Transaction Control Language (TCL):** It allows you to deal with the transaction of the database. Example— Commit, Rollback, Savepoint, Set Transaction.

## WHAT IS MySQL AND ITS FEATURES

MySQL is an open-source RDBMS that works on many platforms. It provides multiuser access to support many storage engines and is backed by Oracle. So, you can buy a commercial license version from Oracle to get premium support services. The features of MySQL are as follows:[3]

- **Ease of Management:** The software can be easily downloaded, and it also has a built-in automatic event scheduler which is very handy when scheduling your tasks.

---

[3] https://www.edureka.co/blog/what-is-mysql/, Edureka

- **Robust Transactional Support:** It is compliant with the Atomicity, Consistency, Isolation, Durability (ACID) property and also allows distributed multi-version support.

- **Comprehensive Application Development:** MySQL has plugin libraries to include the database in any application. It also supports stored processes, triggers, functions, views, and many more for application development.

- **High Performance:** The database can provide fast load utilities with distinct memory caches and table index partitioning.

- **Low Total Cost of Ownership:** Low costs reduce licensing costs and hardware expenditures.

- **Open Source and 24/7 Support:** This RDBMS can be used on any platform and it comes with 24/7 support for open source and enterprise edition.

- **Secure Data Protection:** MySQL supports powerful mechanisms to secure that only authorized users have access to the databases.

- **High Availability:** MySQL can run high-speed master/slave replication configurations and it offers cluster servers.

- **Scalability and Flexibility:** With MySQL you can easily manage deeply embedded applications and make up data warehouses holding a massive amount of information.

Now, that you are more or less familiar with what is MySQL, you should take a look at the various data types supported by it:[4]

- **Numeric:** This data type includes integers of various sizes, floating-point of various precisions, and formatted numbers.

- **Character string:** These data types have either a fixed or a varying number of characters. This data type also has a variable-length string called CHARACTER LARGE OBJECT (CLOB) which is used to specify columns that have large text values.

- **Bit string:** These data types are of either a fixed length or varying length of bits. There is also a variable-length bit string data type called BINARY LARGE OBJECT (BLOB), which is available to specify columns that have large binary values, such as images.

- **Boolean:** This data type stand for TRUE or FALSE values. Since SQL has NULL values, a three-valued logic is used, which is UNKNOWN.

- **Date and Time:** The DATE data type has YEAR, MONTH, and DAY in the form YYYY-MM-DD. Similarly, the TIME data type has the components HOUR, MINUTE, and SECOND in the form HH:MM:SS. These formats can change based on the requirement.

---

[4] https://www.edureka.co/blog/what-is-mysql/, Edureka

- **Timestamp and Interval:** The TIMESTAMP data type includes a minimum of six positions, for decimal fractions of seconds and an optional WITH TIME ZONE qualifier in addition to the DATE and TIME fields. The INTERVAL data type mentions a relative value that can be used to increment or decrement an absolute value of a date, time, or timestamp.

## MySQL MAJOR FEATURES

MySQL is available in two different editions: the open-source MySQL Community Server and the proprietary Enterprise Server. MySQL Enterprise Server is characterized by a series of proprietary extensions which install as server plugins, but otherwise have the version numbering system, and are built from the same code foundation.

There are certain basic features that are available in MySQL untouched since the very first version:

- A broad subset of ANSI SQL 99 as well as extensions

- Cross-platform support

- Stored procedures (SPs), using a procedural language that closely adheres to SQL/PSM

- Triggers

- Cursors

- Updatable views

- Online DDL when using the InnoDB Storage Engine

- Information schema

- Performance Schema that collects and aggregates statistics about server execution and query performance for monitoring purposes

- A set of SQL Mode options to control runtime behavior, including a strict mode to better adhere to SQL standards

- X/Open XA distributed transaction processing (DTP) support; two-phase commit as part of this, using the default InnoDB storage engine

- Transactions with savepoints when using the default InnoDB Storage Engine. The NDB Cluster Storage Engine also supports transactions

- ACID compliance when using InnoDB and NDB Cluster Storage Engines

- SSL support

- Query caching

- Sub-SELECTs (i.e., nested SELECTs)

- Built-in replication support

- Asynchronous replication: master–slave from one master to many slaves or many masters to one slave

- Semi-synchronous replication: master-to-slave replication where the master waits on replication

- Synchronous replication: Multi-master replication is provided in MySQL Cluster.

- Virtual Synchronous: Self-managed groups of MySQL servers with multi-master support can be done using Galera Cluster or the built-in Group Replication plugin.

- Full-text indexing and searching

- Embedded database library

- Unicode support

- Partitioned tables with the pruning of partitions in the optimizer

- Shared-nothing clustering through MySQL Cluster

- Multiple storage engines, allowing one to choose the one that is most effective for each table in the application

- Native storage engines InnoDB, MyISAM, Merge, Memory (heap), Federated, Archive, CSV, Blackhole, and NDB Cluster

- Commit grouping, gathering multiple transactions from multiple connections together to increase the number of commits per second

- The developers release minor updates of the MySQL Server approximately every 2 months. The sources can be obtained from MySQL's website or from MySQL's GitHub repository, both under the GPL license.

MySQL supports various fixed-length and variable-length string types as well as different Statements and Functions. You can see full operator and function support in the SELECT list and WHERE clause of queries. To illustrate:

```
mysql> SELECT CONCAT(first_name, ' ',
last_name)
    -> FROM citizen
    -> WHERE income/dependents > 10000 AND
age > 20;
```

Additionally, database provides full support for the following:

- Full support for SQL GROUP BY and ORDER BY clauses. Support for group functions (COUNT(), AVG(), STD(), SUM(), MAX(), MIN(), and GROUP_CONCAT())

- Support for LEFT OUTER JOIN and RIGHT OUTER JOIN with both standard SQL and ODBC syntax

- Support for aliases on tables and columns as required by standard SQL

- Support for DELETE, INSERT, REPLACE, and UPDATE to return the number of rows that were changed (impacted) or to return the number of rows matched instead by setting a flag when connecting to the server

- Support for MySQL-specific SHOW statements that retrieve information about databases, storage engines, tables, and indexes. Support for the INFORMATION_SCHEMA database implemented according to standard SQL

- Support for EXPLAIN statement to display how the optimizer resolves a query

MySQL also supports the independence of function names from table or column names. Meaning that the only restriction is that for a function call, no spaces are permitted between the function name and the "(" that goes after it. Thus, you can refer to tables from different databases in the same statement.

In terms of security, there is a great privilege and password system that is very versatile yet secure and that enables host-based confirmation. As well as that, there is password security by encryption of all password traffic once you connect to a server.

## SCALABILITY AND LIMITS

MySQL is perfect to support large databases. You can easily use MySQL Server for databases that contain 50 million records that are up to 200,000 tables and about 5,000,000,000 rows. You can extend your data to support for up to 64 indexes per table, while each index may consist of 1–16 columns or parts of columns. An index may use a prefix of a column for CHAR, VARCHAR, BLOB, or TEXT column types. Just to compare, the maximum index width for InnoDB tables is either 767 bytes or 3072 bytes. And the maximum index width for MyISAM tables is 1000 bytes.

MySQL is known for its great connectivity. Thus, clients can connect to MySQL Server using several protocols or by applying TCP/IP sockets on any platform.

On Windows systems, users can connect using named pipes, so once the server is started with the named_pipe, the system variable gets activated. Windows servers also support shared-memory connections if started with the shared_memory system variable enabled. Users also have the option of connecting through shared memory by using the --protocol=memory variable. On Unix systems, you can get connected just by using Unix domain socket files.

MySQL client programs can be scripted in many languages. A client library written in C is available for clients written in C or C++, or for any language that has C bindings. APIs for C, C++, Eiffel, Java, Perl, PHP, Python, Ruby, and Tcl are also available, enabling MySQL clients to be able to operate in many languages.

The Connector built-in interface provides MySQL support for client programs that have Open Database Connectivity connections. For instance, you can use MS Access to link to your MySQL server while running on Windows or Unix at the same time. All ODBC 2.5 functions are supported, as are many others. The additional Connector/J interface provides MySQL support for Java client programs that use JDBC connections. MySQL

Connector/NET enables developers to easily create .NET applications that require unlimited, high-performance data connectivity with MySQL. It also executes the required ADO.NET interfaces and integrates them into ADO. NET aware tools. With this, developers can build applications using their choice of .NET languages as MySQL Connector/NET is a fully managed ADO.NET driver that is written in 100% C#.

In terms of localization potential, the server can provide error messages to clients in a variety of languages. There is also full support for several different character sets, including latin1, german, big5, ujis, several Unicode character sets, and others. To illustrate, even the Scandinavian characters "å," "ä," and "ö" are allowed in table and column names.

All data inserted is saved in the chosen character set. Sorting and comparisons are performed according to the default character set and collaboration. Moreover, it is possible to modify this characteristic once the MySQL server is started. MySQL Server also supports many different character sets that can be identified at compile-time and runtime. With it, the server time zone can be changed dynamically, and individual users can set their own time zone.

As for client-related tools, MySQL includes several client and utility systems. These include both command-line programs such as mysqldump and mysqladmin as well as graphical programs like MySQL Workbench that we shall cover within this chapter only.

MySQL Server has built-in support for SQL statements to review, optimize, and restore tables. These statements are obtainable from the command line through the mysqlcheck client. MySQL also has myisamchk, a very fast command-line toolset for completing these operations on MyISAM tables. As an option, MySQL programs can be called upon with the --help or -? option to obtain online assistance.

MySQL Workbench introduction has to start with the simple notion describing it as a visual database design tool that incorporates SQL development, management, database design, production, and maintenance into a single integrated development environment for the MySQL database system.

The first-ever version of MySQL Workbench was launched in September 2005 but was not included in the MySQL Graphical User Interface Tools Bundle. Development was rolled again in 2007, and MySQL Workbench was announced to become the MySQL Graphical User Interface flagship product. Version numbering was started at 5.0 to assert that MySQL Workbench was created as the successor to DBDesigner4.

- **MySQL Workbench 5.0 and 5.1:** MySQL Workbench 5.0 and 5.1 are both specialty-based visual database design tools for MySQL. While MySQL Workbench 5.0 was an MS Windows-only product, cross-platform support was included in MySQL Workbench 5.1 and so on.

- **MySQL Workbench 5.2:** Starting from MySQL Workbench 5.2, the application has turned into a general database user interface application. Apart from physical database modeling, it has an SQL

Editor, database migration tools, and a database server administration interface, taking over the old MySQL User Interface Tools Bundle.

- **MySQL Workbench 6.0:** In May 2013, the MySQL Workbench Team announced that they were working on version 6.0. The first public beta was consequently released in June 2013, and the first general-availability release was made in August 2013.

- **MySQL Workbench 6.1:** In January 2014, the MySQL Workbench Team released its first public beta of version 6.1. The first open-source availability release was made in March 2014. New items include improved Visual Explain layout, a Performance dashboard, Performance Schema support, additional query result views, and Microsoft Active Accessibility support.

- **MySQL Workbench 6.2:** In August 2014, the MySQL Workbench Team announced its first public beta release of version 6.2. The first general-public release was made in September 2014. New features include shortcut buttons for customary operations such as optional results tab; Microsoft Access Migration; MySQL Fabric Integration; Spatial View Panel to visualize spatial and geometry data; Geometry Data Viewer; ResultSet Width; SQL editor tabs are properly saved; Shared Snippets; a new Run SQL Script dialog; Model Script Attachments; performance columns can display sizes in KB, MB, or GB; the migration wizard can resume operations of data copying if interrupted, and MySQL connection password is now remembered across all the MySQL Workbench session.

• **MySQL Workbench 6.3:** In March 2015, the MySQL Workbench Team announced its first public beta release of version 6.3. The first general-availability release was made later in April 2015. New features include[5] a migration open data from the command line instead of the User Interface, a Secure Sockets Layer certificate generator, improved SQL auto-completion, a new table data import and export wizard, and MySQL Enterprise Firewall support.

• **MySQL Workbench 8.0:** In April 2018, the MySQL Workbench Team announced the first public release of version 8.0.11 as a Release Candidate together with MySQL Community Server 8.0.11. The first general-availability release was issued in July 2018 together with the server following the new policy for the interoperable version numbers across most MySQL products. MySQL Workbench now uses ANTLR4 backend parser and has a new auto-completion engine that runs with object editors (for example, triggers, views, SPs, and functions) in the visual SQL editor and models. Moreover, the new version adds support for new language features in MySQL 8.0, such as common table expressions and roles. There is also support for invisible indexes and persisting of global system variables. The new default authentication

---

[5] https://dev.mysql.com/doc/workbench/en/wb-what-is-new-63.html, MySQL

plugin caching_sha2_password in MySQL 8.0 is now established by Workbench, so resetting user accounts to other authentication methods is no longer needed when linking to the latest servers. Administrative tabs are upgraded with the latest configuration options, and the user interface was made more flexible between the tabs.

Prominent features of MySQL Workbench are[6]

- Database Connection and Instance Management

- Wizard driven action items

- Fully scriptable with Python

- Support for custom plugins

- Windows Accessibility API compliant

- Supports MySQL Enterprise features (Audit Log, Firewall, and Enterprise Backup)

- SQL Editor

- Schema object browsing, inspection, and search

- SQL syntax highlighter and statement parser

- SQL code completion and context-sensitive help

- Multiple and editable result sets

- Visual EXPLAIN

---

[6] https://dev.mysql.com/doc/workbench/en/wb-what-is-new.html, MySQL

- SQL snippets collections

- Secure Socket Shell (SSH) connection tunneling

- Unicode support

- Data modeling

- ER diagramming

- Drag'n'Drop visual modeling

- Reverse engineering from SQL Scripts and live database

- Forward engineering to SQL Scripts and live database

- Schema synchronization

- Printing of models

- Import from fabFORCE.net DBDesigner4

- Database administration

- Start and stop of database instances

- Instance configuration

- Database account management

- Instance variables browsing

- Logfile browsing

- Data dump export/import

- Performance monitoring

- Performance Schema metrics

- MySQL instance dashboard

- Query statistics

- Database migration

- Any ODBC compliant database

- Native support: Microsoft SQL Server, PostgreSQL, SQL Anywhere, SQLite, and Sybase ASE

At the same time, MySQL Workbench is the very first MySQL family of products that offer two different editions—an open-source and a proprietary edition. The "Community Edition" is a full-featured product that is not distorted in any way. Being the foundation for all other editions, it has benefited from all the other development efforts. The proprietary "Standard Edition" extends the Community Edition with a series of modules and plugins.

However, like any other relational database system, MySQL database server also has its advantages and disadvantages. Some of these advantages include the following:

- **Reduced total cost of ownership:** MySQL is one of the most popular open-source database management systems that let you manage relational database all by yourself. Since MySQL is open source, you can use MySQL freely, and if you need to, it is possible to tailor its source code according to your specific requirement. Most of the companies opt particularly for MySQL because this way they do not have to pay anything for this great product.

- **Portability:** MySQL is a cross-platform database server meaning that it can run on different platforms such as Linux, Solaris, Windows—just to name a few. Therefore, it is an excellent choice for those projects that target multiple platform–based web applications. As a matter of fact, we have already mentioned that MySQL is a part of the LAMP (Linux Apache MySQL PHP) server stack which is applied worldwide for web application development. In addition to the portability notion, MySQL supports many platforms with different languages like C, C++, PHP, PERL, JAVA, and Python.

- **Seamless Connectivity:** There are various secure and smooth connection methods that are available in order to get access to the MySQL server. The most generally used tools include named pipes, TCP/IP sockets, and UNIX Sockets. Additionally, the database provides robust development and round-the-clock uptime that comes with the assurance of 24/7 uptime and offers a wide range of high-availability tools, including specialized cluster servers and master/slave replication options. To keep these up-to-date, MySQL maintains a very large developer community that is committed to examining and releasing regular repairs and updates for MySQL.

- **Data Security:** MySQL is globally recognized as the most secure and reliable database management system that is out there in popular web applications including WordPress, Drupal, Joomla, Facebook, and Twitter. The data that MySQL holds is protected via passwords in encrypted forms that cannot be broken even by the most complex encryption algorithms.

MySQL compatibility factor is derived from the fact that it supports SQL as its standardized language for querying and updating data as well as for the administration of a database. At the same time, there are several SQL dialects (almost as many as there are database systems). MySQL complies to the current SQL standard (at the moment SQL:2003), although with a few restrictions and a large number of necessary extensions. Through the configuration setting SQL-mode, you can make the MySQL server operate for the most part compatibly with various other database systems. Among these are IBM DB/2 and Oracle.

By and large, the fact that MySQL supports the following key tools also counts as one of its main advantages:

- **Since version 4.1:** MySQL is capable of processing a query in the form SELECT * FROM table1 WHERE x IN (SELECT y FROM table2) (Including other numerous syntax variants for subSELECTs).

- **Views:** To put it simply, views relate to an SQL query that is processed as a distinct database object and makes available a particular view of the database. MySQL has worked with views since version 5.0.

- **SPs:** This item is mostly dealing with SQL code that is stored in the database system. SPs are typically used to simplify particular steps, such as inserting and removing a data record. For user programmers, this comes as an advantage since they do not have to process the tables directly anymore but can rely on SPs. Similar to views, SPs assist in the management of major database projects. SPs were applied in order to increase efficiency since version 5.0.

- **Triggers:** Triggers are SQL commands that are automatically activated by the server in certain database operations (INSERT, UPDATE, and DELETE). MySQL has supported triggers in a limited quantity also since version 5.0.

- **Unicode:** MySQL has supported all of the conceivable character combinations since version 4.1, including Latin-1, Latin-2, and Unicode (both variants UTF8 and UCS2).

- **User interface:** There are a number of optional convenient user interfaces to choose from for easy administering of a MySQL server.

- **Full-text search:** Full-text search clarifies and accelerates the search for words and phrases that are placed within a text field. If you apply MySQL for storing text (let's say for an Internet discussion group), you can use full-text search to complete a simple and efficient search function.

- **Replication:** Replication allows the contents of a database to be duplicated (copied) onto a number of other devices. In practice, this is activated for two main reasons: to increase protection against any potential system failure (so that if one computer goes down, another can be put to facilitate the failure) and to improve the overall rate of database queries.

- **Transactions:** In the frame of a database system, a transaction stands for the execution of several database operations as a block. The database system makes sure that either all of the operations are rightfully executed or none of them. This could be called upon, even if in the middle of a transaction there is a power failure, the machine crashes, or some other damage happens. Thus, for instance, it cannot be possible that a sum of money is withdrawn from account A but fails to be transferred in account B because of some type of systemic error.

Transactions also give programmers a chance to interrupt a series of already implemented commands (a sort of revising). In many cases, this would lead to a serious simplification of the programming process. In spite of popular opinion, MySQL has supported transactions for a long time. It is also important to mention that MySQL can store tables in a variety of formats. The default table format is called MyISAM, and this format does not support transactions, but apart from it, there are many other additional formats that do support transactions. The most popular of them is InnoDB, which will be described in the final chapter of this book.

- **Foreign key constraints:** These are certain regulations that make sure that there are no cross-references in linked tables that lead to nowhere. Thus, MySQL supports foreign key constraints for InnoDB tables.

- **Geographic information systems (GIS) functions:** Since version 4.1, MySQL has supported the storing and processing of two-dimensional geographical data making it a well-suited tool for GIS application.

- **Programming languages:** There is a variety of different application programming interfaces and libraries for the development of MySQL applications. For beginner programming, you can use, among others, the languages C, C++, Java, Perl, PHP, and Python.

- **ODBC:** As mentioned, MySQL supports the ODBC interface Connector/ODBC. This allows MySQL to be addressed by all the usual programming languages that run under Microsoft Windows (such as Delphi, Visual Basic). The ODBC interface can also be implemented under Unix, though that is rarely needed. Windows programmers who have transferred to Microsoft's new .NET platform can, if they need to, make use of the ODBC provider or the .NET interface Connector/NET.

- **Platform independence:** It is not only client applications that can work under a variety of operating systems but also MySQL server that can be administered under a number of operating systems. The most widely used are Apple Macintosh OS X, Linux, Microsoft Windows, and a number of Unix variants, such as AIX, BSDI, FreeBSD, HP-UX, OpenBSD, Net BSD, SGI Iris, and Sun Solaris.

## DISADVANTAGES

Nevertheless, the MySQL database server has its disadvantages. Some of these disadvantages include the following:

- MySQL early versions (5.0 or less) do not support ROLE, COMMIT SPs.

- MySQL does not support a very large database size as efficiently. Or simply, MySQL is simply not for large-sized data. At the same time, MySQL works perfectly fine in most small or medium applications, but when data grows in size, the performance gets significantly worse. When that happens, only the simple and indexed query maintains good performance, and for a complicated query, it easily gets slow sometimes even unable to meet the request in the feasible time-frame. Therefore, you need to carefully design your SQL query to keep its availability no matter what.

  In case you expect your application to grow very big in size at some point in the future, you need to rethink the decision of using MySQL as your database at all. Because it may work fine at the beginning, until one day when you need to scale it. Thus, you may want to consider diversifying the data, that is, distributing data from one table to other multiple locations and machines. But at the same time, MySQL does not support auto-sharing, meaning you would have to maintain the nodes manually. And in case you would need an auto-failover, you should request an external utility or start writing your own script. We do not claim it to be impossible to make it scale, but it would probably take some serious engineering effort to make it work. Difficulties related to MySQL scalability are mostly pushing users to switch to NoSQL databases like MongoDB.

- MySQL does not manage transactions very efficiently, and it is prone to data corruption.

- MySQL does not have an accomplished developing and debugging tool compared to other databases.

- MySQL does not support SQL check constraints.

- MySQL is owned by Oracle. Meaning that even though MySQL is an open-source product, not that it is acquired by Oracle that has total control of the software, it makes many developers feel uncomfortable about the situation, to say the least. Some of them have turned to MariaDB because of that. As mentioned before, when Oracle acquires Sun Microsystem, MySQL which belongs to Sun was sold to Oracle too. Oracle database is mainly applied in enterprises and big corporations, so it has an obvious dominance in that domain, but MySQL still stands as one of their competitors. Oracle published an official statement about keeping MySQL competitive but did not specify any deadline to that promise. That only means that if one day Oracle may choose to weaken MySQL, that is, acquire to kill in the future, it will freely be able to do so. On the other hand, it can also decide to actually improve MySQL to make it better, treating it like its own product. There are several uncertainties as such discussed out there in the developers' community.

Speaking of specific MySQL technical limitations, one should start by getting to know Identifier Length Limits. Here you can get to know the maximum length for each type of identifier:[7]

| Identifier Type | Maximum Length (Characters) |
|---|---|
| Database - | 64 (Network Database storage engine: 63) |
| Table - | 64 (Network Database storage engine: 63) |
| Column - | 64 |
| Index - | 64 |
| Constraint - | 64 |
| Stored program - | 64 |
| View - | 64 |
| Table space - | 64 |
| Server - | 64 |
| Log file group - | 64 |
| Alias - | 256 |
| Compound statement label - | 16 |

It is also worth mentioning that aliases for column names in CREATE VIEW statements are checked against the maximum column length of 64 characters (not the maximum alias length of 256 characters).

For constraint definitions that are not composed of any constraint name, the server internally creates a name that comes from the associated table name. For instance, internally produced foreign key constraint names consist of the table name as well as _ibfk_ and a number. If the table

---

[7] https://dev.mysql.com/doc/refman/5.6/en/identifier-length.html, MySQL

name is close to the length-approved potential for constraint names, the additional characters necessary for the constraint name may cause that name to exceed the limit, ending up in an error.

Identifiers are stored in their specified Unicode (UTF-8). This also extends to identifiers in table definitions that are stored in .frm files and to identifiers that are located in the grant tables in the MySQL database. The sizes of the identifier string columns in the grant tables are regulated in characters. You can use multibyte for these items without having to reduce the number of characters allowed for values stored in these columns.

Next, one would have to look at the Grant Table Scope Column Properties limitations. Scope columns in the grant tables hold strings. The default value for each one of those is the empty string. Here you can see the exact number of characters permitted in each column:[8]

| Column Name | Maximum Permitted Characters |
|---|---|
| Host, Proxied_host - | 60 |
| User, Proxied_user - | 16 |
| Password - | 41 |
| Table_name - | 64 |
| Column_name - | 64 |
| Routine_name - | 64 |

Here, Host and Proxied_host values should be converted to lowercase prior to being stored in the grant tables. As per access-checking standards, comparisons of User, Proxied_user, Password, and Table_name values are case-sensitive.

---

[8] https://dev.mysql.com/doc/mysql-reslimits-excerpt/5.7/en/grant-tables-scope-column-properties.html, MySQL

Yet comparisons of Host, Proxied_host, Column_name, and Routine_name values are not case-sensitive.

At the same time, MySQL has no limit on the number of databases, but the overall file system might have a limit on the number of directories. And while MySQL has no limit on the number of tables, the basic file system might have a limit on the number of files that represent tables. Additionally, individual storage engines may also impose engine-specific constraints. Thus, InnoDB allows no more than 4 billion tablets.

Another limitation would be that of table size. The effective maximum table size for MySQL databases is typically set by operating system capacity for file sizes and not by MySQL internal constraints. If you do not know your information operating system file size limits yet, you might want to refer to the documentation specific to your operating system.

Windows users should also note that File Allocation Table and Virtual File Allocation Table (FAT32) are not considered acceptable for production use with MySQL. You would have to use New Technology File System designed mostly for journaling instead. If any full-table error occurs, there are several reasons why you might have encountered it:

- You have run out of an operating system file size limit. For instance, you are using MyISAM tables on an operating system that accommodates files only up to 2GB in size, and you have met this limit for the data file or index file.

- The disk should be full.

- You are using InnoDB tables and might not have any spare room left in an InnoDB tablespace file. The maximum tablespace size is also the maximum size for a table. Typically, in that case, partitioning of tables into multiple tablespace files is recommended for tables larger than 1TB in size.

- You are using a MyISAM table and the space required for the table is much bigger than what is allowed by the internal pointer size. MyISAM lets data and index files grow up to 256TB by default, but this limit can be modified up to the maximum permissible size of 65,536TB (2567—1 bytes).

However, in case if you MUST use a MyISAM table that is larger than the default limit and your operating system supports large files, the CREATE TABLE statement supports AVG_ROW_LENGTH and MAX_ROWS options that the server uses to determine how large a table to permit. And in case the pointer size is too small for an existing table, you can edit those options with ALTER TABLE to increase a table's maximum allowed size with the following statement:

```
ALTER TABLE tbl_name MAX_ROWS=1000000000
AVG_ROW_LENGTH=nnn;
```

Make sure you specify AVG_ROW_LENGTH only for tables with BLOB or TEXT columns so that in this case, MySQL will not be able to optimize the space required based only on the number of rows.

Another thing you can do to change the default size limit for MyISAM tables is to set the myisam_data_pointer_size, which defines the number of bytes used for internal row pointers. The value is applied to determine the pointer size for new tables if you do not include the MAX_ROWS option. The value of myisam_data_pointer_size can range from 2 to 7. For instance, for tables that are based on the dynamic storage format, a value of 4 allows to place tables up to 4GB; a value of 6 permits tables up to 256TB. Tables that incorporate the fixed storage format have a larger maximum data length. You should be able to check the maximum data and index sizes by using this statement:

```
SHOW TABLE STATUS FROM db_name LIKE
'tbl_name';
```

In addition, it is also possible to use myisamchk -dv/path/ to/table-index-file.

Other ways to work around file size limits for MyISAM tables are the following:

- If your large table is to read-only, you can include myisampack in order to try and compress it. myisampack normally compresses a table by at least 50%, so you can have, as a result, much bigger tables. myisampack can also merge multiple tables into a single table.

- MySQL has a built-in function of a MERGE library that enables you to administer a collection of MyISAM tables that have the same structure as a single MERGE table.

Another thing to consider is Column Count Limitation. MySQL has a hard limit of 4096 columns per table, but the assertive maximum may be less for a given table. The precise column limit depends on the following factors:

- Storage engines may have their own additional restrictions that limit table column count. To illustrate, InnoDB has a limit of 1017 columns per table.

- Each table has an .frm file that contains the table definition. The definition impacts the content of this file in ways that may affect the number of columns allowed in the table.

- The storage requirements of individual columns constrain the number of columns that suit a given maximum row size. Storage requirements for particular data types depend on things like storage engine, storage format, and character set.

Similar thing with Row Size Limits, the maximum row size for a given table mainly depends on several factors. Firstly, the internal capacity of a MySQL table can hold a maximum row size limit of 65,535 bytes, even if the storage engine allows more supporting larger rows. BLOB and TEXT columns can only contribute 9–12 bytes toward the row size limit due to their contents that are stored separately from the rest of the row.

Next, the maximum row size for an InnoDB table, which manages the data stored locally within a database page, can only be slightly less than half a page. For instance, the maximum row size is slightly less than 8KB for the default 16KB InnoDB page size, which is determined by the innodb_page_size configuration variable.

And at last, If a row containing variable-length columns gets over the InnoDB maximum row size, InnoDB opts for variable-length columns for external off-page storage until the row can be placed within the InnoDB row size limit. The amount of data put down locally for variable-length columns that are stored off-page varies depending on the row format. Thus, different storage formats can govern different amounts of page header and trailer data, which directly affects the amount of storage available for rows.

Now that we know the basic features and limitations that MySQL contains, it is time to learn how to install, configure, and access MySQL via the command line, and we shall be doing just that in the next chapter.

# CHAPTER 2

# Getting Started with MySQL

➤ Describing how to install MySQL database

➤ Figuring out how to create and manage MySQL connection

➤ Learning how to access the MySQL via the Command

In this chapter, we are going to describe how to obtain and install MySQL. A notion of the procedure will be mentioned in later chapters as well. Yet it is generally recommended to start the installation following the steps outlined:

First, you need to decide whether MySQL operates and is supported on your platform. This one is because not all platforms are suitable for running MySQL, and not all platforms on which MySQL is known to operate are officially supported by Oracle Corporation.

Second, you need to choose which distribution to install. There are several versions of MySQL available out there, and most are available in several distribution arrangements. You can select from pre-packaged distributions containing binary (or precompiled) programs or from source code. In addition, Oracle provides access to the MySQL source code for those who just want to see recent upgrades and test new code. Thus, while preparing to install MySQL, decide which version and distribution format (binary or source) to turn to.

After that, one has to determine whether to install a development release or a General Availability (GA) release. Development releases tend to have the newest features but are not recommended for production use. On the other hand, GA releases are sometimes called production releases, meaning they are perfect for production use.

When shopping for MySQL, pay attention to the naming scheme. In MySQL 8.0, the release names consist of three numbers and an optional suffix (e.g., MySQL-8.0.1-dmr). The numbers within the release name have the following interpretation:

- The first number (8) is the major version number.

- The second number (0) is the minor version number. A combination of the major and minor numbers will give you the release series number that describes the stable feature set.

- The third number (1) is the version number within the release series. This is upgraded with each new bugfix release.

Release names usually also have a suffix to indicate the stability level of the release. Releases within a series progress through a set of suffixes to show how the stability level increases. The widely used suffixes are **dmr** stands for a development milestone release. MySQL development applies a milestone model, in which each milestone has a small subset of thoroughly tested features. From one milestone to the next, feature interfaces may evolve, or features may even be canceled, based on feedback provided by community developers who tested these early releases.

RC stands for a Release Candidate. RCs are thought to be stable, having passed all of MySQL's testing levels. New features might be introduced in RC releases, but the focus more likely is to fixing bugs or improve features introduced earlier within the series.

The absence of a suffix means you are looking at a GA or Production release. GA releases are stable, having successfully passed through the earlier release stages, and are believed to be relatively clean from serious bugs, and perfect for use in production plans. Normally, development within a series starts with DMR releases, followed by RC releases, and finally reaches GA status releases.

Once you choose which MySQL version to install, you should select the distribution format to install for your operating system. For most cases, a binary distribution is the simplest option. Binary distributions are accessible in native format for many platforms, such as RPM packages for Linux or DMG packages for macOS. Distributions are also obtainable in more widely used formats such as Zip archives or compressed tar files. On Windows, you can even use the MySQL Installer to install a binary distribution.

Sometimes, it may also be preferable to install MySQL from a source distribution. This option is reserved in case you might want to install MySQL at some explicit location or you might require even more flexibility to place MySQL items where you want.

Additionally, you want to modify mysqld with features that might not be native to the standard binary distributions. The most common extra options used to ensure feature availability include

- DWITH_LIBWRAP=1 for TCP wrappers support

- DWITH_ZLIB={system|bundled} for characteristics that depend on compression

- DWITH_DEBUG=1 for debugging procedure

Thus, only after you have downloaded the distribution that you want, you can perform any necessary post-installation setup. In the next section, we are going to provide instructions for installing MySQL on different platforms and environments available on a platform-by-platform basis: Unix, Linux/FreeBSD/Microsoft Windows/macOS.

## INSTALLING AND CONFIGURING

Installing MySQL on Unix/Linux

As a rule, Oracle provides a set of binary distributions of MySQL. These include generic binary distributions in the form of compressed tar files (files with a .tar.xz extension) for a number of platforms and binaries in platform-specific parameters for selected platforms.

This section is a brief explanation of the MySQL installation from a compressed tar file binary distribution on Unix/Linux platforms. Normally, MySQL compressed tar file binary distributions have names of the form MySQL-VERSION-OS.tar.xz, where VERSION is a number (e.g., 8.0.25), and OS indicates the type of operating system for which the distribution is intended.

There is also a "minimal install" version of the MySQL compressed tar file for the Linux generic binary distribution, which has a name of the form MySQL-VERSION-OS-GLIBCVER-ARCH-minimal.tar.xz. The minimal install distribution does not include debug binaries and is stripped of debug items, making it significantly smaller than the regular binary distribution. If you decide to install the minimal install distribution, you need to make sure to adjust for the difference in file name format in the instructions that follow. Thus, in order to install a compressed tar file binary distribution, unpack it at the installation location of your choice (typically/usr/local/MySQL). This creates the following basic directories:[1]

| Directory | Contents of Directory |
| --- | --- |
| Bin - | MySQL server, client, and utility programs |
| Docs - | MySQL manual in Info format |
| Man - | Unix manual pages |
| Include - | Include (header) files |
| Lib - | Libraries |
| Share - | Error messages, dictionary, and SQL for database installation |
| support-files - | Miscellaneous support files |

Also worth mentioning that debug versions of the MySQL binary are accessible at the MySQL-debug file. To create

---

[1] https://dev.mysql.com/doc/refman/8.0/en/binary-installation.html, MySQL

your own debug version of MySQL from a source distribution, you can apply the appropriate configuration options to activate debugging support.

It might be the case that your system does not natively have a user and group to use for operating mysqld, thus you need to create them. The following commands add the MySQL group and the MySQL user. You might need to require the user and group instead of MySQL. If so, the syntax for useradd and groupadd may differ slightly on different versions of Unix/Linux, or they may have different names such as adduser and addgroup. To illustrate:

```
shell> groupadd MySQL
shell> useradd -r -g MySQL -s/bin/false
MySQL
```

Here, since the user is required only for ownership grounds, not login means, the useradd command has the -r and -s/bin/false variables to create a user that does not have login permissions to your server host. You can always leave out these options if your useradd does not support them.

To obtain and unpack the distribution you should select the directory under which you are going to unpack the distribution and change the location into it. The example here unpacks the distribution under /usr/local. The instructions, therefore, assume that you are allowed to create files and directories in/usr/local. If that directory is not available, you are expected to perform the installation as root: shell> cd/usr/local

When you unpack the distribution, it creates the installation directory. tar that further uncompresses and unpacks the distribution if it has z option support:

```
shell> tar xvf /path/to/mysql-VERSION-OS.
tar.xz
```

The tar command also produces a directory named MySQL-VERSION-OS.

To install MySQL from a compressed tar file binary distribution, your system must have GNU XZ utilities to uncompress the distribution and a suitable tar to unpack it. Thus, you should download and install GNU tar (http://www.gnu.org/software/tar/), or at least use a preinstalled version of GNU tar. Usually, this is available under gnutar, gtar, or as tar within a GNU or Free Software directory, such as /usr/sfw/bin or /usr/local/bin.

In case your tar does not support the xz format then insert the xz command to unpack the distribution and tar to unpack it. With it, replace the previous tar command with the following alternative command to uncompress and extract the distribution: shell> xz -dc /path/to/mysql-VERSION-OS.tar.xz | tar x

Next, stabilize a symbolic link to the installation directory created by tar: shell> ln -s full-path-to-MySQL-VERSION-OS MySQL

The ln command in here creates a symbolic link to the installation directory. This lets you refer more easily to it as /usr/local/MySQL. To avoid having to type the pathname of client programs always when you are working with MySQL, you can insert the /usr/local/MySQL/bin directory to your PATH variable shell> export PATH=$PATH:/usr/local/MySQL/bin

The post-installation setup process only includes setting distribution ownership and access permissions, initializing the data directory, and starting the MySQL server.

### Installing MySQL on FreeBSD

This section provides guidance on installing MySQL on FreeBSD Unix.

You can install MySQL on FreeBSD by utilizing the binary distribution provided by Oracle. However, the easiest way to install MySQL for newbies is to use the MySQL-server and MySQL-client ports available at http://www. freebsd.org/. Using these ports gives you the following advantages:

- A working MySQL with all optimizations enabled is thought to work on any version of FreeBSD.

- Automatic configuration option.

- Startup scripts installed in /usr/local/etc/rc.d.

- The ability to use pkg_info -L command to see which files are installed.

- The ability to use pkg_delete command to remove MySQL if it is no longer necessary.

- Be able to access prerequisite libraries as per ldd mysqld: libthr, libcrypt, libkrb5, libm, librt, libexecinfo, libunwind, and libssl.

The MySQL build process requires GNU make (gmake) to work. If you do not have GNU yet, you must install it first before compiling MySQL.

If you wish to install the database using the ports system, use the following set of commands:

```
# cd /usr/ports/databases/mysql80-server
# make
```

The standard port installation would then locate the server into /usr/local/libexec/mysqld, with the startup script for the MySQL server placed in /usr/local/etc/rc.d/mysql-server.

If you need to remove MySQL after installation using the ports system insert the following:

```
# cd /usr/ports/databases/mysql80-server
# make deinstall
```

## Installing MySQL on Microsoft Windows

The easiest and most recommended method is to download MySQL Installer and let it install and modify a specific version of MySQL Server as follows:

First, download MySQL Installer from https://dev.mysql.com/downloads/installer/ and implement it. Note that, unlike the standard MySQL Installer, the smaller web-community version does not include any MySQL applications, but downloads only the MySQL items you select to install.

Next, opt for the setup type to use for the initial installation of MySQL products:

- **Developer Default:** Provides a setup type that has the selected version of MySQL Server as well as other MySQL tools related to MySQL development, such as MySQL Workbench.

- **Server Only:** Provides a setup for the selected version of MySQL Server without other products.

- **Custom:** This lets you select any version of MySQL Server and other MySQL products.

With that, MySQL is now installed. If you set MySQL as a service, then Windows will automatically start the MySQL server every time you restart the system. This process also installs the MySQL Installer application on the localhost, which can later be used to upgrade or reconfigure the MySQL server. In addition, if you installed MySQL Workbench on your system, you might consider using it to check your new MySQL server connection. By default, the program automatically runs after installing MySQL.

*Additional Installation Information*

You can also run MySQL as a standard application or as a Windows service. By choosing a service, you can monitor and track the operation of the server through the basic Windows service management tools.

To activate the RESTART statement, the MySQL server forks run as a service or standalone, to enable supervision of the server process. In case of RESTART capability is not required, the server can be started with the no-monitor option. Nevertheless, you should install MySQL on Windows using an account that has administrator rights. Otherwise, you might have issues with certain operations such as editing the PATH environment variable or accessing the Service Control Manager. When installed,

MySQL does not have to be executed using a user with Administrator privileges.

In addition to the MySQL Server package, you may need or want additional components to use MySQL with your application or development environment. These include, but are not limited to:

```
Connector/ODBC driver and Connector/NET
driver.
```

Even though MySQL for Windows is available in several distribution formats, it is still recommended to use MySQL Installer. Since it contains more features and MySQL products than the older MSI, it is easier to use than the compressed file, and you do not need any additional tools to get MySQL running. MySQL Installer automatically installs MySQL Server as well as creates an options file, starts the server, and enables you to create various user accounts. It also includes MySQL Workbench, MySQL for Visual Studio and can be used to upgrade all the above-mentioned products in the future (https://dev.mysql.com/doc/mysql-compat-matrix/en/).

The standard binary distribution (presented as a compressed file) has all of the necessary files that you unpack into your chosen location. This package holds all of the data in the full Windows MSI Installer package, yet it does not include an installation program. The source distribution format has all the code and support files for producing the executables using the Visual Studio compiler system.

In addition, if you require tables with a size larger than 4GB, you should install MySQL on an NTFS or newer file system. Do not forget to insert MAX_ROWS and AVG_ROW_LENGTH when you create tables.

## MySQL and Virus Checking Software

It is typical for virus-scanning software such as Norton/Symantec Anti-Virus containing MySQL data and temporary tables to cause issues, both in terms of the operation of MySQL and the virus-scanning software misinterpreting the contents of the data. This is due to the fingerprinting system utilized by the virus-scanning software, and the way in which MySQL swiftly updates its data, which may be perceived as a potential security risk.

Therefore, once you install MySQL Server, it is recommended that you disable virus scanning on the main directory (datadir) used to collect your MySQL data. There is usually a mechanism built into the virus-scanning software to make sure some directories are omitted.

By default, MySQL also produces temporary folders in the standard Windows temporary directory. To prevent the temporary files from being scanned, they are configured into a separate temporary directory for MySQL, this way, they are placed into the virus scanning exclusion list. To do this, you should add a configuration option for the tmpdir parameter to your my.ini configuration file.

During the initial setup process, you are prompted to choose the MySQL products to be installed on the host. A good decision would be to go with the predetermined setup type that suits your setup requirements. By default, both GA and pre-release products are included in the download and installation with the Developer Default, Client only, and Full setup types. You can opt for the Only install GA products option to limit the product set to include GA products only when using these setup types. Choosing one of the following setup types regulates the initial installation only and does not limit your ability to install or update MySQL the following products for Windows later on:

- MySQL Shell
- MySQL Router
- MySQL Workbench
- MySQL for Visual Studio
- MySQL Connectors (for .NET / Python / ODBC / Java / C++)
- MySQL Documentation
- MySQL Samples and Examples

In the next section, we shall describe the MySQL Installer product catalog, the dashboard, and other items related to production operations.

The product catalog is used to store the complete list of released MySQL items for Microsoft Windows that are available to download from MySQL Downloads. By default, MySQL Installer updates the catalog at startup every seven days, but if you wish you can also update the catalog manually from the dashboard. An up-to-date catalog performs carries out the following actions:

> populates the Available Products pane of the Select Products page and adds operation from the dashboard.

In addition, the catalog includes all development releases (Pre-Release), general releases (Current GA), and minor releases (Other Releases). Products in the catalog typically vary depending on the MySQL Installer release that you go for.

MySQL Installer dashboard is the default setting that you see once you start MySQL Installer after the initial setup is complete. If you closed MySQL Installer before the setup was over, MySQL Installer will go on with it before it displays the dashboard. Products covered under Oracle Lifetime Sustaining Support, are usually presented on the dashboard. These products, such as MySQL for Excel and MySQL Notifier, are added automatically, yet can be modified or removed.

MySQL Installer dashboard Elements have a variety of actions that apply to installed products or products displayed in the catalog. To commence the following operations, you should click on the operation link and then select the product or products to manage. The operation "Add" proceeds to the Select Products page. From there, you can regulate the filter, choose one or more products to download, and start the installation. Here, you can use the directional arrows to move each product from the Available Products column to the Products To Be Installed column. To enable the Product Features page where you can customize features, click the related check box.

For MySQL Server earlier versions, the account you utilize to run MySQL Installer may not have adequate permission to install the server data, therefore, interrupting the installation process because the ExecSecureObjects MSI action cannot be implemented. To disable that, deselect the Server data files feature before trying to install the server again.

Even though the Server data files check box was removed from MySQL Server 8.0. and higher you can still perform the following actions freely:

- **Modify:** You should use this operation to add or delete the items associated with installed products. Features that you can edit typically differ in complexity by product. When the Program Shortcut check box is selected, the product shall be displayed in the Start menu under the MySQL group.

- **Upgrade:** This operation will load the Select Products to Upgrade page and add all the upgrade features to it. An installed product can have more than one upgrade version and the operation requires a current product catalog. MySQL Installer upgrades all of the chosen products in one action. You can click on the Show Details option to view the actions performed by MySQL Installer.

- **Remove:** This operation enables the Remove Products page and occupies it with the MySQL products located in the host. You should select the MySQL products you want to remove and then click Execute to start the removal procedure. During the operation, an indicator will show the number of steps that are implemented as well as a percentage of all steps. In order to select products to remove, you can either select the check box for one or more products or click the Product check box to select all products.

There is also the reconfigure link in the Quick Action column next to each installed server loads that show current configuration values for the server and then cycle through all configuration steps allowing you to change the options and values. You should provide credentials with root privileges to reconfigure these items. Click the Log tab to show the output of each configuration step performed by MySQL Installer. Once completed, MySQL Installer stops the server, applies the configuration updates, and then restarts the server. Installed Samples and Examples associated with a specific MySQL server version can also be remodified to apply new feature settings.

The Catalog link lets you download the latest catalog of MySQL products manually and then consolidate those product changes with MySQL Installer. The catalog-download option does not activate an upgrade of the products already installed on the host. Rather, it returns to the dashboard and inserts an arrow icon to the Version column for each installed product that has a newer version. You can later use the Upgrade operation to install the newer product version.

You can also apply the Catalog link to see the current change history of each product without having to download the new catalog. Just click on the Do not update at this time check box to view the change history.

The MySQL Installer About icon displays the current version of MySQL Installer and general information about MySQL. The version number is located above the Back button. Remember to include this version number when reporting a problem with MySQL Installer at all times. In addition to the About MySQL information you can also choose the following icons from the side panel:

- **License icon for MySQL Installer:** This solution includes third-party software, used under license. If you are operating with a Commercial release of MySQL Installer, the icon calls for the MySQL Installer Commercial License Information User Manual for licensing information, presenting licensing information relating to third-party software that may be included in this Commercial release. In case you are using a Community release of MySQL Installer, the icon shows the MySQL Installer Community License Information User Manual for licensing information, including licensing information relating to third-party software that may be included in this Community release.

  Resource links icon is responsible for displaying the latest MySQL product documentation, blogs, and webinars.

The MySQL Installer Options icon includes information about the following tabs:

- **Product Catalog:** Administers the automatic catalog updates. As already mentioned, MySQL Installer checks for catalog updates at startup every seven days. When new products or product versions are available, MySQL Installer includes them in the catalog and then adds an arrow icon next to the version number of the installed products list. It is also possible to use the product catalog option to enable or disable automatic updates and to change the number of days between automatic catalog downloads. Meaning, MySQL

Installer will use the number of days you set to see whether a download should be attempted or not.

- **Connectivity Settings:** Several operations completed by MySQL Installer need Internet access. This option lets you use a default value to check the connection or to use a different URL, one selected from a list or added by you manually. With the Manual option selected, new URLs can be tested, and all URLs in the list can be validated or removed. When the Automatic option is activated, MySQL Installer tries to connect to each default URL in the list until a connection is made. If no connection can be established, it results in an error.

MySQL products in the catalog are located by different categories:[2] MySQL Servers, Applications, MySQL Connectors, and Documentation. Only the latest versions have the function of the Available Products by default. If you need to see a pre-release or older version of a product, it may not be available in the default list. Anyway, it is important to keep the product catalog updated. You can click Catalog on the MySQL Installer dashboard to download the latest manifest.

In case you want to edit the default product list, click Add in the dashboard to open the Select Products page, and then click Edit to open the dialog box. You can then modify the settings and then click Filter. You should be able to see the data filtered by Text, Category, Maturity, Already Downloaded, and Architecture.

---

[2] https://dev.mysql.com/doc/workbench/en/wb-mysql-connections-secure-auth.html, MySQL

Moreover, you can reset one or more of the following fields to modify the list of available products:

- **Category:** Stands for all Software, MySQL Servers, Applications, MySQL Connectors, or Documentation.

- **Maturity:** Indicates current version, Pre-Release or Other Releases. In case any warning appears, just confirm that you have the most recent product manifest by clicking Catalog on the MySQL Installer dashboard.

In the meantime, the Commercial release of MySQL Installer does not show any MySQL products when you select the Pre-Release maturity filter. Products in development are accessible from the Community release of MySQL Installer only.

Already Downloaded option allows you to view and administer downloaded products only. However, MySQL Installer does not allow server upgrades between major release versions or minor release versions but does permit upgrades within a release series, such as an upgrade from 5.7.11 to 5.7.12. Upgrades between milestone releases are not supported, but major development changes can take place in milestone releases.

For upgrades to MySQL 8.0.16 server and higher, a check box option lets you skip the upgrade check and process directly for system tables while processing data dictionary tables in the background. MySQL Installer does not bring about the check box when the previous server upgrade was skipped or when the server was modified as a sandbox InnoDB Cluster. This pattern represents a change in how MySQL Server completes an upgrade and advances the sequence of steps that MySQL Installer takes to the configuration process.

To select a new server version just Click Upgrade. Make sure that the check box next to the product name in the Upgradeable Products section has a checkmark. Deselect the products that you do not need to be upgraded at the time. For server milestone releases in the same release series, MySQL Installer deselects the server upgrade and shows a warning saying that the upgrade is not supported, as well as provides a summary of the steps to take in order to perform the upgrade manually.

Meanwhile, if you click on a product, it not only highlights it but also populates the Upgradeable Versions with the details of each available version for the selected product: version number, published date, and a Changes link to see the release notes for that version.

In order to remove a local MySQL server, first, decide whether the local data directory should be removed. If you keep the data directory, another server installation can reapply the data. This option is activated by default. You can click Execute to begin uninstalling the local server but keep in mind that all products that you selected to remove will also uninstall at this time.

MySQL Installer stays installed on your computer and can be upgraded from the previous version. Sometimes, other MySQL software may request for you to upgrade MySQL Installer for better compatibility. To identify the current version of MySQL Installer and upgrade MySQL Installer manually you need to first locate the installed version of MySQL Installer.

Start MySQL Installer from the search menu. Once the MySQL Installer dashboard opens, just click the MySQL Installer About icon. The version number would be displayed above the Back button.

To start an on-demand upgrade of MySQL Installer follows this order:

- Connect the computer with MySQL Installer installed to the Internet

- Start MySQL Installer from the search menu. The MySQL Installer dashboard opens

- Click Catalog on the bottom of the dashboard to open the Update Catalog window

- Click Execute to begin the process. If the installed version of MySQL Installer can be upgraded, you will be prompted to start the upgrade

- Click Next to review all changes to the catalog and then click Finish to return to the dashboard

- Verify the installed version of MySQL Installer

## Installing MySQL on macOS

Even before you start installing MySQL on macOS you should keep the following notions in mind:

- **Other MySQL installations:** The installation procedure does not support MySQL installations by package managers such as Homebrew. The installation and upgrade procedures are coming strictly from MySQL package providers. If there are any other installations, then consider canceling them before implementing the installer to prevent any port conflicts from happening.

- **Homebrew:** In case you installed MySQL Server using Homebrew to its default location, then the MySQL installer downloads to a different location and will not upgrade the version from Homebrew. If that happens, you might end up with multiple MySQL installations that, by default, will be using the same ports. Thus, to prevent errors from occurring, you need to stop the other MySQL Server instances before running this installer.

- **Launched:** A launchd daemon is installed in order to alter MySQL configuration options. You might need to consider editing it prior MySQL installation.

- **Users:** You may want to create a particular MySQL user to own the MySQL directory and data. You can do this through the Directory Utility, and the MySQL user should already exist. For use in single-user mode, an entry for _mysql should already exist within the system /etc/passwd file.

- **Data:** Because the MySQL package installer holds the MySQL contents into a version and platform-specific directory, you can apply this to upgrade and move your database between versions. You need to copy the data directory from the old version to the new version, or to specify an alternative datadir value to set the location of the data directory.

- **Aliases:** You might need to include aliases to your shell's resource file to make it easier to access commonly practiced programs such as MySQL and mysqladmin from the command line.

The syntax for bash is:[3]

```
alias mysql=/usr/local/mysql/bin/mysql
alias mysqladmin=/usr/local/mysql/bin/
mysqladmin
```

And for tcsh, use

```
alias mysql/usr/local/mysql/bin/mysql
alias mysqladmin/usr/local/mysql/bin/
mysqladmin
```

Moreover, you can add /usr/local/MySQL/bin to your PATH environment variable just by modifying the appropriate startup file for your shell.

- **Removing:** After you have duplicated the MySQL database files from the previous installation and have successfully activated the new server, you should think about deleting the old installation files to save disk space. In addition, you should also get rid of the older versions of the Package Receipt directories located in /Library/Receipts/MySQL-VERSION.pkg.

## Installing MySQL on macOS Using Native Packages

The Native package is placed inside a disk image file that you first should organize by double-clicking its icon in the Finder. It should then mount the image and display its contents. Before starting the installation, you would need to stop running MySQL server instances by using either

---

[3] https://dev.mysql.com/doc/mysql-macos-excerpt/5.7/en/macos-installation-notes.html, MySQL

the MySQL Manager Application, the preference pane, or mysqladmin shutdown variable in the command line.

To install MySQL using the package installer, you need to first download the disk image (.dmg) file that holds the MySQL package installer. Then double-click the file to check the disk image and see through its contents. Double-click the MySQL installer package from the disk that is named according to the version of MySQL you have downloaded. For instance, for MySQL server 8.0.25 it might be named MySQL-8.0.25-macOS-10.13-x86_64.pkg.

The initial wizard introduction screen references the MySQL server version to install. Click Continue to begin the installation. The MySQL community edition will then present a copy of the relevant GNU General Public License. Click Continue and then Agree to continue. From the Installation Type page, you can click Install to start the installation wizard using all defaults, and then click Customize to modify which components to install. However, even if the Change Install Location option is available, the installation location still cannot be changed.

After that click Install to install MySQL Server. After a successful new MySQL Server installation, complete the configuration steps by choosing the default encryption type for passwords, define the root password, and also enable or disable MySQL server at startup. The default MySQL 8.0 password mechanism is caching_sha2_password, and this step permits you to change it to mysql_native_password. Most content is described in the surrounding text. To be precise, the installer refers to caching_sha2_password as "Use Strong Password Encryption" and mysql_native_password as a "Use Legacy Password Encryption."

Selecting the legacy password mechanism advances the generated launchd file to set --default_authentication_plugin=mysql_native_password under Program Arguments. Choosing strong password encryption does not set default_authentication_plugin because the default MySQL Server value is utilized, which is caching_sha2_password.

You should also choose a password for the root user and decide whether MySQL Server should start after the configuration step is over. A summary is the final stage and references a successful MySQL Server installation. You can now close the wizard.

MySQL server is now installed. If you wish not to start MySQL, then use either launchctl from the command line or start MySQL by clicking "Start" using the MySQL preference pane. When installing using the package installer, the files are installed into a directory within /usr/local matching the name of the installation version and platform. For instance, the installer file MySQL-8.0.25-macos10.15-x86_64.dmg installs MySQL into /usr/local/MySQL-8.0.25-macos10.15-x86_64/ with a symlink to /usr/local/MySQL.

Here you can see the layout of this MySQL installation directory. However, the macOS installation process does not create nor install a sample my.cnf MySQL configuration file.

| Directory | Contents of Directory |
| --- | --- |
| Bin- | mysqld server, client and utility programs |
| Data- | Log files, databases, where /usr/local/MySQL/data/mysqld.local.err is the default error log |
| Docs- | Helper documents, like the Release Notes and build information |
| Include- | Include (header) files |

*(Continued)*

| Directory | Contents of Directory |
|---|---|
| Lib- | Libraries |
| Man- | Unix manual pages |
| MySQL-test- | MySQL test suite ('MySQL Test' is disabled by default during the installation process when using the installer package (DMG)) |
| share- | Miscellaneous support files, including error messages, dictionary.txt, and rewriter SQL |
| support-files- | Support scripts, such as mysqld_multi.server, MySQL.server, and MySQL-log-rotate. |
| /tmp/MySQL.sock- | location of the MySQL Unix socket |

# CREATING AND MANAGING CONNECTIONS

This section describes how to create and administer MySQL connections.

For starters, in order to create a new connection, you have to follow these steps:

First, launch MySQL Workbench to open the home screen. Existing connections will be displayed when you click the MySQL Connections view from the sidebar. No connections will exist for first-time users. Following the MySQL Workbench home screen shown in the previous figure, click the [+] icon near the MySQL Connections label to view the Setup New Connection wizard.

Next, you need to define the Connection Name value, such as MyFirstConnection. The default connection values are for a typical local setup, so you must review them and then enter the appropriate values. If you are unsure, you can always click the Test Connection button to check the connection parameters.

After that, you may optionally click Configure Server Management, which calls up the Configure Local Management wizard. Here you are required to read the Configure Local Management introduction and press Next to begin defining the new connection standards. The connection will now be tested. You should be able to see whether that connection was successful and if not, click Back and check that you have entered the information correctly.

You should then be able to view additional details about the tested connection, and click Next. Alternatively, you can modify a method for remote management if a Remote Host was specified. Setting these options lets MySQL Workbench set the location of configuration files, and the correct start and stop commands to use for the connection.

The Secure Shell (SSH) login-based management and Native Windows remote management types are both available within the database framework. The Operating System and MySQL Installation Type can therefore be configured for the SSH login type. This step results in a local MySQL connection, so you can skip the Management and OS and SSH Configuration options, which are used for setting a remote MySQL connection.

To start with, on Microsoft Windows, pick the appropriate MySQL service for the MySQL connection. The wizard will then check its ability to access the start and stop commands and then check access to the MySQL Server configuration file.

You now have a chance to review the configuration settings. The information presented differs slightly depending on the platform, connection, and installation type. At the Review Settings menu, select the one that says "I'd like to review the settings again." Here you can check the Change Parameters if you want to check or edit information about the MySQL configuration file. As an alternative, you can insert your own commands for starting, stopping, and checking the MySQL connection. To apply the default values, keep these optional values blank, click Finish to close the Configure Server Management dialog, and return to the original Setup New Connection step.

After reviewing the Setup New Connection information just click Test Connection again to make sure it still functions and then click OK to create the new MySQL connection. Your new MyFirstConnection MySQL connection will now be listed on the home screen.

From the home screen, click the new MySQL connection to open the SQL editor for this connection. The SQL editor is the default page. Click Server Status from the Navigator area of the sidebar to display the current status of the connected MySQL server instance. Test the other Navigator area options that relate to your new MySQL connection. See its status, MySQL logs, and measure its performance statistics from the dashboard.

In the Navigator area, you can see the Administration and Schemas tabs. The Schemas view shows all the schemas that are incorporated into your new MySQL connection. Alternatively, you can unite the content of the tabs by either clicking merge or by enabling the Show Management Tools and Schema Tree in a single tab SQL editor preference.

The Manage Server Connections dialog is another great way to keep your MySQL tidy. This dialog is called upon by either clicking the manage connections icon on the home screen or by selecting Database and then Manage Connections from the main menu. It can also be activated from any of the wizards requiring access to a live database.

After the MySQL connection manager is launched, you shall have the Connection tab of the Manage Server Connections dialog. The most important elements of the MySQL Connection Manager include the following:[4]

- **Connection Name:** The name used to refer to this connection. This connection can then be selected from a list in other wizards requiring a connection.

- **Connection Method:** Method used to connect to the RDBMS.

- **New button:** Opens a separate Manage Server Connections dialog to make a new connection. This dialog has two tabs in addition to the Connection tab: Remote Management and System Profile

- **Delete, Duplicate, Move Up, and Move Down buttons:** Operations used to administer the existing connections.

---

[4] https://dev.mysql.com/doc/workbench/en/wb-manage-server-connections. html, MySQL

- **Test Connection button:** Tests the selected MySQL connection and reports the connection status. It also reports whether or not SSL is enabled. For testing remote connections, you might also need to check the hostname, or check the port. If these fail, then also check the firewall settings on each host, and also that MySQL server is running on the remote host.

- **Simultaneous client connections:** Opening a MySQL connection from the MySQL Workbench home screen opens a new connection tab in MySQL Workbench for that connection. Each of these tabs has to have two MySQL connections to complete basic tasks, such as schema discovery and SQL execution. Moreover, performing management-related tasks, such as Server Status, requires two additional MySQL connections. Basically, this means that each MySQL connection tab in MySQL Workbench needs to have four available connections to MySQL.

Mainly, this connection requirement doubles with each connection tab opened in MySQL Workbench, even if the two connection tabs are related to the same MySQL server. SQL editor tabs share their connections, so having multiple SQL editor and SQL results tabs does not really impact the number of necessary connections.

### Standard TCP/IP Connection Method

This connection method makes it possible for MySQL Workbench to connect to MySQL Server using TCP/IP.

At the same time, the skip_networking MySQL system variable impacts the TCP/IP connection method. If disabled, use named pipes or shared memory (on Windows) or Unix socket files (on Unix).

The parameters for standard TCP/IP connections are[5]:

- **Hostname:** The hostname or IP address of the MySQL server.

  - The hostname "localhost" might resolve to "127.0.0.1" or "::1" on your host, so note this when checking permissions. To demonstrate, if a web application's user only has access to "127.0.0.1" on a host, and a defined connection uses "localhost" that resolves to "::1," this connection might not have the proper permissions to the web application. Add "localhost" variable to each host to determine where it resolves to.

- **Port:** The TCP/IP port on which the MySQL server is sitting (the default is 3306).

- **Username:** User name to use for the connection.

- **Password:** Optional password for the account used. If you enter no password here, you will be prompted to enter the password when MySQL Workbench attempts to establish the connection. In addition, MySQL Workbench can store the password in a vault.

---

[5] https://dev.mysql.com/doc/workbench/en/wb-manage-server-connections. html, MySQL

- **Default Schema:** When the connection to the server is made, this is the schema that will be used by default. It becomes the default schema for use in other parts of MySQL Workbench.

Also, you might be expected to establish a Secure Sockets Layer Tab (SSL). SSL parameters are[6]

- **Use SSL:** This dropdown provides options related to enabling SSL encryption. Choose No to disable SSL, If available if the client library supports it, or Require to require SSL support for the MySQL connection to succeed.

- **SSL Key File:** Path to the Key file for SSL.

- **SSL CERT File:** Path the Certificate file for SSL.

- **SSL CA File:** Path to the Certification Authority file for SSL.

- **SSL Cipher:** Optional list of permissible ciphers to use for SSL encryption.

- **SSL Wizard button:** Generate SSL certificates for both the MySQL server and MySQL client. Requires access to OpenSSL binaries in the system's PATH. Files button: Opens a file browser that points to the generated SSL files by the SSL Wizard.

---

[6] https://dev.mysql.com/doc/workbench/en/wb-manage-server-connections.html, MySQL

The Advanced tab includes these checkboxes:[7]

- **Use compression protocol:** If checked, the communication between the application and the MySQL server will be compressed, which may increase transfer rates. This corresponds to starting a MySQL command-line client with the --compress option. This option is unchecked by default.

- **Use ANSI quotes to quote identifiers:** Treat """" as an identifier quote character (like the "`" quote character) and not as a string quote character. You can still use "`" to quote identifiers with this mode enabled. With this option enabled, you cannot use double quotation marks to quote literal strings, because it is interpreted as an identifier. However, if this option is checked, it overrides the server setting. This option is unchecked by default.

- **Enable Cleartext Authentication Plugin:** Send the user password as text that is not encrypted. Required for some authentication methods. This option is unchecked by default.

- **Timeout:** Maximum time to wait before the connection is aborted. The connection times out in 60 seconds by default.

- **SQL_MODE:** Override the default SQL_MODE used by the server.

---

[7] https://dev.mysql.com/doc/workbench/en/wb-manage-server-connections. html, MySQL

- **Others:** Other options for Connector/C++ as option=value pairs, one per line.

- **Standard TCP/IP over SSH Connection Method:** This connection method enables MySQL Workbench to connect to MySQL Server using TCP/IP over an SSH connection.

In addition to a number of parameters that are in common with Standard TCP/IP connections, this connection method has a number of specialized parameters. These items are:

- **SSH Hostname:** The name of the SSH server. An optional port number can also be provided. For example, localhost:22.

- **SSH Username:** The name of the SSH user to use to make a connection.

- **SSH Password:** The SSH password. It is recommended that an SSH key file is also used.

- **SSH Key File:** A path to the SSH key file.

At the same time, MySQL Workbench does not accept default PuTTY keys directly. Yet, you can convert an existing PuTTY Private Key (PPK) file to OpenSSH format using the PuTTY Key Generator (PuTTYGen) utility.

In another case, if a remote host is missing from the system's list of familiar hosts, a prompt shall ask you to confirm the host's fingerprint before storing it. If your stored host fingerprint does not match the host's current fingerprint, then an error is produced, and you will be required to manage the discrepancy from outside of MySQL Workbench before establishing the connection. On Linux and macOS, SSH host fingerprints are stored in ~/.ssh/known_hosts. On Microsoft Windows, they are stored in a file created by MySQL Workbench under the user's folder, such as C:\ Users\username\.ssh\known_hosts.

*Configuring Server Management Wizard*

Clicking the [+] item from the home screen activates the Setup New Connection wizard. The wizard provides a MySQL connection form to make a new MySQL connection and includes a Configure Server Management option as a step-by-step method for establishing a new MySQL server connection.

This option can also be implemented later from the home screen by clicking the top right corner of a MySQL remote connection. Executing this wizard is necessary to complete tasks requiring shell access to the host. For instance, starting/stopping the MySQL instance and modifying the configuration file.

The steps presented in the wizard are

- **Test DB Connection:** On this page, MySQL Workbench checks your database connection and offers the results. If an error pops out, just click Show Logs to see the related logs.

- **Management and OS:** Applied to specify a remote management type and pick out the operating system, which is available when the Host Machine is treated as a remote host.

Furthermore, the SSH login-based management option includes configuration entries for the Operating System and MySQL Installation Type.

## SSH Configuration

If you defined a Remote Host on the Specify Host Machine page, you will be forwarded to the Host SSH Connection page, which lets you use SSH for the connection to the server instance. This facility enables you to establish a secure connection to remotely manage and configure the server instance. You must fill in the hostname and user name of the account that will be utilized to log in to the server for administration and configuration activities. If you do not enter the optional SSH Key for use with the server, then you will be demanded the password when the connection is created by MySQL Workbench.

This connection is made to authorize remote administration and configuration of the MySQL Server itself. It is not similar to the connection used to connect to a server for general database manipulation. You must need an SSH connection type when administering a remote server if you want to start or stop the server configuration process. Apart from that, other administrative functions do not require an SSH connection.

## Windows Management

If a Windows server is utilized, then setting the Windows configuration parameters is obligatory. Windows management searches for a user account with the required privileges to query the system status, and to control services.

And read/write access to the configuration file is mandatory to permit editing of the file.

With that, the wizard shall attempt a connection to your server and immediately report the results. If an error occurs, click Show Logs to view the related logs.

Besides, MySQL Workbench should know where the MySQL Server configuration file is placed to be able to prepare some configuration information. The wizard is able to define the most likely placement of the configuration file, based on the selection made on the Operating System page of the wizard. Nevertheless, it is possible to test that this data is correct by clicking the Check path and Check section buttons. The wizard then reports whether the configuration file and server configuration section can in fact be reviewed. It is also possible to manually select the location of the configuration file, and the section specified to MySQL Server data; these manually inserted values should be tested using the buttons provided. Here just click the Next button to continue.

*Review Settings*

The modified settings may be evaluated, which also includes the default values. Choose the Change Parameters check box if the MySQL Config File section will be edited and then click Next to continue.

*MySQL Config File*

Enables configuration of the MySQL server version. It also permits the editing and validation of the configuration file path and validation of the server instance section. Here just click Next to continue.

*Specify Commands*

Optionally prop the commands required to start, stop, and examine the status of the running MySQL server instance. Commands can be edited if needed, but the defaults are satisfactory in most cases. The defaults depend on the chosen options on the Operating System page of the wizard. Click Next to continue.

*Complete Setup*

In this final step, you are required to name the MySQL server instance. This name will be used throughout MySQL Workbench as a reference to this MySQL connection. After setting an appropriate name, click Finish to save the instance.

*The Password Storage Vault*

The vault stands for useful secure storage for passwords applied to access MySQL servers. By using the vault, you need not insert the same credentials every time MySQL Workbench tries to connect to a server. The hostname is used for storing password data. For instance, a local connection might use "localhost," "127.0.0.1," or "::1," but these are stored separately in the password storage vault, even if they all generated in the same place.

The vault is executed differently on each platform:

- **Windows:** The vault is an encrypted file in the MySQL Workbench data directory. This is where connections.xml and related files are placed. The file is encrypted using a Windows API which operates the encryption based on the current user, so only the current user can decrypt it. As a result, it is not possible to decrypt the file on any other computer. It is possible to remove the file, in which case all stored passwords are gone, but MySQL Workbench will otherwise operate as usual. You then should re-enter passwords as expected.

- **macOS:** The vault is executed using the Secure Keychain. The keychain data is also available from the native Keychain Access.app utility.

- **Linux:** The vault operates by storing passwords using the libsecret library, which interacts with Secret Service. For systems with the GNOME desktop environment, such as Ubuntu, the Secret Service is gnome-keyring-daemon. Systems with the KDE desktop environment, for instance, Kubuntu, apply their own secret service implementation.

*Updating Old Authentication Protocol Passwords*

MySQL 4.1 extended password average between 16 and 41 bytes. However, upgrading MySQL does not automatically update the old password passwords, so previous passwords are still located in the deprecated format. This is because MySQL does not store passwords as plain text, so regenerating password requires direct user involvement.

Upgrading a password does have certain limitations. Here are two options to choose from:

If the secure_auth MySQL Server option is unavailable, then you can log in using the user with the old password format and update the user's own MySQL password. But this is not an option for MySQL Workbench 6.3.5 because compatibility with the old password format was deleted. Because of that, a user's capacity to upgrade their own password format must be done using the MySQL command line.

In case using the MySQL command line is not an option, then you can use an older version of MySQL Workbench (from version 6.3.4 and earlier), which lets you enable a Use the old authentication protocol option under the Advanced connections tab. You can see older versions of MySQL Workbench are available at https://downloads.mysql.com/archives/workbench/.

As mentioned earlier, secure_auth is enabled by default as of MySQL 5.6 and MySQL 5.7. If secure_auth is enabled, you cannot log in to your user's password that is stored in the old format. Attempts will not work and result in an error similar to "ERROR 2049 (HY000): Connection using old (pre-4.1.1) authentication protocol refused (client option 'secure_auth' enabled)." In order to upgrade the password, you can either disable secure_auth then update it, or log in as a different user, such as root, to change the password for a different user.

*Using MySQL Workbench to Upgrade Your Password*
In regards to everything stated above, there are two methods to update passwords using MySQL Workbench. To start, open the Users and Privileges tab from the Management navigator. Select the user account you want to update from the User Accounts section. If inserting the old password format, you will see text beginning with "This account is using the pre-MySQL-4.1.1 password hashing type." in the

lower right corner of the screen, and also a large Upgrade button on the right. From here, you can

- **Option for all MySQL versions:** Manually insert a new password, or the current password, and click Upgrade. This upgrades the password to the newer password format, and the MySQL user can now log in using the new password.

- **Option for MySQL 5.6 and later:** Instead of editing the password field, leave it as it is and immediately click Upgrade. From here, you can create a random password and tag it as expired by clicking Reset To Expired. Use this temporary random password to log in the user, and MySQL will ask you for a new password when the user first logs in.

## ACCESSING THE MySQL VIA THE COMMAND

This section narrates options supported by most MySQL client systems that control how client programs create connections to the server, whether connections are encrypted, or whether connections are compressed. These options can be divided by three different command lines:

- Command Options for Connection Establishment

- Command Options for Encrypted Connections

- Command Options for Connection Compression

Command Options for Connection Establishment[8]

| Option Name | Description |
|---|---|
| default-auth - | Authentication plugin to use |
| host - | Host on which MySQL server is located |
| password - | Password to use when connecting to server |
| pipe - | Connect to server using named pipe (Windows only) |
| plugin-dir - | Directory where plugins are installed |
| port - | TCP/IP port number for connection |
| protocol - | Transport protocol to use |
| shared-memory-base-name - | Shared-memory name for shared-memory connections |
| socket - | Unix socket file or Windows named pipe to use |
| user - | MySQL user name to use when connecting to server |

- **default-auth=plugin:** A regulation about which client-side authentication plugin to use.

- **host=host_name, -h host_name:** The host on which the MySQL server is running. The value can be treated like a hostname with an IPv4 address or IPv6 address. The default value is localhost.

---

[8] https://dev.mysql.com/doc/refman/8.0/en/connection-options.html, MySQL

- **password[=pass_val], -p[pass_val]:** The password of the MySQL account selected for connecting to the server. The password value is optional. If not chosen, the program demands one by default. If inserted, there must be no space between --password= or -p and the password following it. If no password option is specified, the default is to send no password.

  Identifying a password on the command line might be considered insecure. To avoid having to give the password on the command line, use an option file. To explicitly state that there is no password and that the client program should not ask for one, use the --skip-password option.

- **pipe:** On Windows, link to the server using a named pipe. This option applies only if the server was activated with the named_pipe system variable enabled to support named-pipe connections. Moreover, the user making the connection should be a member of the Windows group specified by the named_pipe_full_access_group system variable.

- **plugin-dir=dir_name:** Stands for a directory in which to search for plugins. Specify this option if the --default-auth option is used to mark an authentication plugin.

- **port=port_num, -P port_num:** For TCP/IP connections, the port number to use. The default port number is 3306.

- **protocol={TCP|SOCKET|PIPE|MEMORY}:** This option specifically states which transport protocol to apply for connecting to the server. It is convenient when other connection parameters normally end up using a protocol other than the one you want. For instance, connections on Unix to localhost are made using a Unix socket file by default:

- **MySQL --host=localhost:** To force TCP/IP transport to be used instead, specify a --protocol option:

- **MySQL --host=localhost --protocol=TCP:** The following list illustrates the permissible --protocol option values and presents the applicable platforms for each value. To note, the values are not case-sensitive.[9]

| Protocol Value | Transport Protocol Used | Applicable Platforms |
|---|---|---|
| TCP | TCP/IP transport to local or remote server | All |
| SOCKET | Unix socket-file transport to local server | Unix |
| PIPE | Named-pipe transport to local server | Windows |
| MEMORY | Shared-memory transport to local server | Windows |

- **shared-memory-base-name=name:** On Windows, the shared-memory name is applied when you need to move shared memory to a local server. The default value is MYSQL. The shared-memory name is case-sensitive. This option would work only if the

[9] https://dev.mysql.com/doc/refman/8.0/en/connection-options.html, MySQL

server was started with the shared_memory system variable that is made to support shared-memory connections.

- **socket=path, -S path:** On Unix, the name of this Unix socket file is used for connections shared a named pipe to a local server. On Windows, this option applies only if the server was started with the named_pipe system variable enabled to support named-pipe connections. Besides, the user making the connection should be a member of the Windows group identified by the named_pipe_full_access_group system variable.

- **user=user_name, -u user_name:** Stands for a user name of the MySQL account to use for connecting to the server. The default user name is ODBC on Windows or your Unix login name on Unix.

## Command Options for Encrypted Connections

These commands could be treated as options for client programs that specify whether to utilize encrypted connections to the server, the names of certificate and key files, and other items related to encrypted connection support. These options have an impact only for connections that use a transport protocol subject to encryption such as:[10]

---

[10] https://dev.mysql.com/doc/refman/8.0/en/connection-options.html, MySQL

| Option Name | Description |
| --- | --- |
| --get-server-public-key | Request RSA public key from server |
| --server-public-key-path | Path name to file containing RSA public key |
| --ssl-ca | File that contains list of trusted SSL Certificate Authorities |
| --ssl-capath | Directory that contains trusted SSL Certificate Authority certificate files |
| --ssl-cert | File that contains X.509 certificate |
| --ssl-cipher | Permissible ciphers for connection encryption |
| --ssl-crl | File that contains certificate revocation lists |
| --ssl-crlpath | Directory that contains certificate revocation-list files |
| --ssl-fips-mode | Whether to enable FIPS mode on client side |
| --ssl-key | File that contains X.509 key |
| --ssl-mode | Desired security state of connection to server |
| --tls-ciphersuites | Permissible TLSv1.3 ciphersuites for encrypted connections |
| --tls-version | Permissible TLS protocols for encrypted connections |

- **get-server-public-key:** Stands for a request from the server the public key required for pair-based password exchange. This option is well suited for clients that authenticate with the caching_sha2_password authentication plugin. For that plugin, the server does not provide the public key unless requested. This option is omitted in accounts that do not authenticate with that plugin. It is also canceled if password exchange is not activated, as is the case when the client accesses the server using a secure connection.

- **server-public-key-path=file_name:** This is a pathname to a file in Privacy Enhanced Mail format holding a client-side copy of the public key needed by the server for pair-based password exchange. This option is great for clients that authenticate with the sha256_password or caching_sha2_password authentication plugin. This option is removed from accounts that do not authenticate with one of those plugins. It is also removed if password exchange is not applied, as is the case when the client accesses the server using a secure connection.

In addition, if --server-public-key-path=file_name is given and determines a valid public key file, it takes precedence over --get-server-public-key. This option is available only if MySQL was activated using OpenSSL.

- **ssl-ca=file_name:** This is a pathname of the Certificate Authority (CA) certificate file in Privacy Enhanced Mail format. The file has a list of verified SSL Certificate Authorities. To make the client not authenticate the server certificate when setting up an encrypted connection to the server, specify neither --SSL-ca nor --SSL-capath. The server still verifies the client according to any applicable requirements initiated for the client account, and it still includes any ssl_ca or ssl_capath system variables included to the server-side. To specify the CA file for the server, just insert the ssl_ca system variable.

- **ssl-capath=dir_name:** Stands for a pathname of the directory that holds all trusted SSL CA certificate files in Privacy Enhanced Mail format. To indicated to the client not to authenticate the server certificate when linking an encrypted connection to the server, specify neither --SSL-ca nor --SSL-capath. The server still validates the client according to any applicable requirements set for the client account, and it still includes any ssl_ca or ssl_capath system variable values set on the server-side.

- **ssl-cert=file_name:** The pathname of the client SSL public key certificate file in Privacy Enhanced Mail format. To determine the server SSL public key certificate file, set the ssl_cert system variable.

- **ssl-cipher=cipher_list:** This command stands for the list of permissible encryption ciphers for connections that apply TLS protocols up through TLSv1.2. If no cipher in the list is affirmed, encrypted connections that apply these TLS protocols do not operate. For better interoperability, cipher_list should be a list of one or more cipher names, divided by colons.

- **ssl-crl=file_name:** The pathname of the file holding up certificate revocation lists (CRL) in Privacy Enhanced Mail format. If neither --ssl-crl nor --SSL-crlpath is supported, no CRL checks are performed, even if the CA path supports certificate revocation lists. To define the revocation-list file for the server, prompt the ssl_crl system variable.

- **ssl-crlpath=dir_name:** The pathname of the directory that contains certificate revocation-list files in Privacy Enhanced Mail format. If neither --ssl-crl nor --SSL-crlpath is supported, no CRL checks are performed, even if the CA path holds certificate revocation lists. To determine the revocation-list directory for the server, insert the ssl_crlpath system variable.

- **ssl-fips-mode={OFF|ON|STRICT}:** Monitors whether to enable FIPS mode on the client-side. The --ssl-fips-mode option differs from other --SSL-xxx options in that it is not applied to create encrypted connections, but rather to affect which cryptographic operations to allow. To illustrate, these --SSL-fips-mode values are permissible:

  - **OFF:** Disable FIPS mode.

  - **ON:** Enable FIPS mode.

  - **STRICT:** Enable "strict" FIPS mode.
    At the same time, if the OpenSSL FIPS Object Module is not available, the only permissible value for --SSL-fips-mode is OFF. In this case, setting --ssl-fips-mode to ON or STRICT pushes the client to come up with a warning at startup and to administer in non-FIPS mode.

- **ssl-key=file_name:** The pathname of the client SSL private key file in Privacy Enhanced Mail format. For better security, you can use a certificate with a key size of at least 2048 bits. If the key file is secured by a passphrase, the client program demands the passphrase. The password should be given interactively as it cannot be stored in a file. If the passphrase is not correct, the program keeps going as if it could not read the key. To designate the server SSL private key file, set the ssl_key system variable.

- **ssl-mode=mode:** This option is used to match the desired security state of the connection to the server. These mode values are acceptable, in order to increase security:

  - **DISABLED:** Set an unencrypted connection.

  - **PREFERRED:** Set an encrypted connection if the server has encrypted connections, falling back to an unencrypted connection if an encrypted connection cannot be produced. This is the default if --SSL-mode is not specified.

    Connections over Unix socket files are not encrypted with a mode of PREFERRED. To enable encryption for Unix socket-file connections, use a mode of REQUIRED or stricter.[11]

  - **REQUIRED:** Set an encrypted connection if the server supports encrypted connections. The connection attempt will not be completed if an encrypted connection is not set properly.

  - **VERIFY_CA:** Like REQUIRED, but additionally validate the server CA certificate against the configured CA certificates. The connection attempt fails if no valid matching CA certificates are selected.

  - **VERIFY_IDENTITY:** Like VERIFY_CA, but additionally operate hostname identity verification by checking the hostname the client applies

---

[11] https://dev.mysql.com/doc/refman/8.0/en/connection-options.html, MySQL

for connecting to the server against the identity in the certificate that the server forwards to the client.

As for MySQL 8.0.12, if the client uses OpenSSL 1.0.2 or higher, the client has to see whether the hostname that it uses for connecting matches either the Subject Alternative Name value or the Common Name value in the server certificate. Hostname identity verification also comes with certificates that identify the Common Name using wildcards. In another case, the client checks whether the hostname that it utilizes for connecting matches the Common Name value in the server certificate. The connection fails if there is those two do not match. For encrypted connections, this option helps avoid any hacker attacks.

It is also important to keep in mind that the hostname identity verification with VERIFY_IDENTITY does not apply to self-signed certificates that are generated automatically by the server or manually using mysql_ssl_rsa_setup. Such self-signed certificates do not hold any server names as the Common Name value.

The --SSL-mode option interrelate with CA certificate options in the following manner:[12]

- If --SSL-mode is not explicitly set otherwise, use of --SSL-ca or --SSL-capath implies --SSL-mode=VERIFY_CA.

- For --SSL-mode values of VERIFY_CA or VERIFY_IDENTITY, --SSL-ca or --SSL-capath is also required,

---

[12] https://dev.mysql.com/doc/refman/8.0/en/connection-options.html, MySQL

to offer a CA certificate that matches the one used by the server.

- An explicit --SSL-mode option with a value other than VERIFY_CA or VERIFY_IDENTITY comes together with an explicit --SSL-ca or --SSL-capath option, producing a warning that no verification of the server certificate is completed, despite a CA certificate option being identified.

To acquire such encrypted connections by a MySQL account, insert CREATE USER to produce the account with a REQUIRE SSL variable, or use ALTER USER for an existing account to include a REQUIRE SSL clause. This causes interrelation attempts by clients that utilize the account to be rejected unless MySQL supports encrypted connections and an encrypted connection can be set.

- **--tls-ciphersuites=ciphersuite_list:** This option determines which cipher suites the client allows for encrypted connections that use TLSv1.3. The value is a list of zero or more colon-separated ciphersuite names. To demonstrate:

```
MySQL --tls-ciphersuites="suite1:suite2:
suite3"
```

The ciphersuites that can be named for this option depend on the SSL library used to come up with MySQL. If this option is not available, the client has to allow the default set of cipher suites. If the option is set to the empty string, no ciphersuites are enabled and encrypted connections cannot be authorized.

- **--tls-version=protocol_list:** This option optimizes the TLS protocols list that the client selects for encrypted connections. The value, therefore, is a list of one or more comma-separated protocol items. To demonstrate:

```
mysql --tls-version="TLSv1.1,TLSv1.2"
```

The protocols that can be named for this option depend on the SSL library applied to compile MySQL. Permitted protocols should be selected such as not to leave free spaces in the list. To illustrate, these values do not have any space in between:

- --tls-version="TLSv1,TLSv1.1,TLSv1.2,TLSv1.3"

- --tls-version="TLSv1.1,TLSv1.2,TLSv1.3"

- --tls-version="TLSv1.2,TLSv1.3"

- --tls-version="TLSv1.3"

These values do have variables skipped in between, therefore should not be used:

- --tls-version="TLSv1,TLSv1.2"

- --tls-version="TLSv1.1,TLSv1.3"

## Command Options for Connection Compression

This section describes options that let client programs monitor the use of compression for connections to the server. The Connection-Compression Option Summary goes the following way[13]:

| Option Name | Description |
| --- | --- |
| --compress | Compact all information sent between client and server |
| --compression-algorithms | Supported compression algorithms for connections to server |
| --zstd-compression-level | Compression level for connections to server that use zstd compression |

- **--compress, -C:** Compress all information exchanged between the client and the server.

- **--compression-algorithms=value:** Stand for all the permitted compression algorithms for connections to the server. The available algorithms operate in a similar manner as the protocol_compression_algorithms system variable. The default value is uncompressed.

- **--zstd-compression-level=level:** Identifies the compression level to apply for connections to the server that uses the zstd compression algorithm. The average level is from 1 to 22, with larger values indicating increasing levels of compression. The default zstd compression level is 3. The compression level setting has no recognized impact on connections that do not use zstd compression.

On the foundation of what we have learned about starting up with MySQL, in the next chapter, we shall look deeper into Data Modeling and Storing Routines of the database.

---

[13] https://dev.mysql.com/doc/refman/8.0/en/connection-options.html, MySQL

# CHAPTER 3

# Data Modeling

## IN THIS CHAPTER

➢ Understanding the main concepts about MySQL data modeling

➢ Learning how to apply stored routines

➢ Managing MySQL reverse engineering processes

Data modeling is the process of operating and analyzing data models for resources located in a database. The data model is an abstract system that standardizes the data specification, data semantic, and consistency limitations of data. Its main aim is to administer the types of data within a structure, the relationships between objects, and their characteristics. The data model helps to recognize what data is necessary and how data should be arranged properly. It is like a guideline for an analyst to better group and catalog what is being created.

DOI: 10.1201/9781003229629-3

The bigger the scope of data circulates in an organization, the more advanced data modeling tool is required. The functionality potential of these tools can be very broad and impressive. Nevertheless, the main features of these tools are the following:

- Compatibility with various models and their levels

- Capacity to produce new models from existing ones

- Management of different data elements

- Support for common modeling activities

- Management of relationships and dependencies between models and their items

- Business glossary

Creating and overseeing a data model requires collaboration among different management areas (data architect, business stakeholders, product-users). The use of data modeling software connects and clears the information flow as well as verifies the correct representation of all data items necessary by the database. Moreover, the tool is great for systemizing the model at three levels: physical, logical, and conceptual. Additionally, it helps when searching for missing and redundant data. The end result of the above advantages is a reduction of very time-consuming data modeling activities and consequently saving resources for the organization.

MySQL is very plentiful when it comes to data types. There are a wide variety of options available to sufficiently store and recapture data. To look back on Chapter 1, these are the data types most commonly used in MySQL:

- INT—For storing integer values
- CHAR—For storing fixed-length character values
- VARCHAR—For storing character values with variable lengths
- DATETIME—For storing date and time information
- TIMESTAMPS—For storing timestamps of various actions
- TEXT—For storing large amounts of text data
- ENUM—For storing one of the preset values
- BOOLEAN—For storing a single Boolean value
- BLOB—For storing binary files and objects

MySQL has its own certain methods when it comes to storing data. MySQL is based on the concepts of tables, columns, and rows. For starters, we need to understand that MySQL data is normally located in isolated environments called databases that are separated from other databases. A database here stands for the topmost entity in MySQL. It contains tables that communicate with each other. But at the same time, a table from one database cannot communicate with a table from another database.

Tables should be viewed as containers for related data. They can also be considered as collections of data that can be grouped and arranged accordingly together. For instance, a table named student could hold data such as name, date of birth, and others. However, it may not be suitable to include data such as an address, house, and other things. For such data, it would make a lot more sense to create a new table. Each data item will then be counted as a column, and a group of such columns would set up a table. Nevertheless, there cannot be two tables with the same name in a database. At the same time, rows contain the veritable data in your database. Each row acts like an entry into a table that pretty much looks like an excel sheet.

Modeling disentangles database design and operability by enabling you, the data manager, to visualize requirements and settle design issues. Model-based database design is a well-structured methodology for producing valid and efficient databases while securing the flexibility to respond to expanding data requirements. Models are applied to build Enhanced entity-relationship (EER) diagrams and physical MySQL databases via visual database design tool MySQL Workbench.

MySQL Workbench provides an extensive set of upgraded features for creating and manipulating database models, including specific tasks such as:

- Creating and exploiting a model graphically

- Reversing engineer, live databases to a model

- Forwarding engineer model to a script or live database

- Creating and modifying tables, inserting multidimensional, multidisciplinary data

## CREATING AND MANAGING TABLES AND RELATIONS

As previously mentioned, tables are the foundation of the organizational structure in SQL databases. They consist of a number of columns that reflect individual patterns of each row, or record, in the table. Being such a primarily important aspect of data organization, it is crucial for anyone who works with relational databases to learn how to create, modify, and delete tables as requested. In this section, we shall cover how to create tables in MySQL, as well as how to edit and delete existing tables.

In order to follow this part, you will need a computer running some type of relational database management system (RDBMS) that uses SQL. The instructions and examples in this guide were certified using the following environment: A server running Ubuntu 20.04, with a non-root user with administrative privileges. And MySQL installed and secured on the server If your SQL database system runs on a remote server, SSH into your server from your local machine:

```
ssh example@your_server_ip
```

Then open up the MySQL server prompt, replacing example with the name of your MySQL user account:

```
MySQL -u example -p
```

Create a database named tablesDB - CREATE DATABASE tablesDB;
   And if the database was created successfully, you should be able to receive output like this:

```
Output - Query OK, 1 row affected
(0.01 second)
```

To select the tablesDB database, run the following USE statement - USE tablesDB;

```
Output - Database changed
```

With that, you are now ready to go with the rest of this chapter and begin learning about how to create and manage tables in MySQL.
   Start by double-clicking the Add table icon in the Physical Schemas section of the Model Overview tab adds a table with the default name of table1. If a table with this name already exists, the new table is named table2.
   Creating a new table automatically opens the table editor that is located at the bottom of the application.

Right-clicking a table opens a context menu with the following items:[1]

```
Cut 'table_name': Cut a table to optionally
paste it into another schema.
Copy 'table_name': Copy a table to
optionally paste it into another schema.
Paste 'table_name': Paste a cut or copied
table. The Paste option is also accessible
from the main Edit menu.
Edit 'table_name': Changes the docked table
editor to the selected table.
Edit 'table_name' in New Tab: Opens the
table in a new table editor tab.
Copy SQL to Clipboard: Copies a CREATE
TABLE statement for the table.
Copy Column Names to Clipboard: Copies a
comma-separated list of column names.
Copy Insert to Clipboard: Copies INSERT
statements based on the model's inserts.
Nothing is copied to the clipboard if the
table has no inserts defined.
Copy Insert Template to Clipboard: Copies
a generic INSERT statement that is based
on the model.
Delete 'table_name': Remove a table from
the database.
```

The last item immediately deletes the table without a confirmation dialog box. If applicable, you can try Remove

---

[1] https://dev.mysql.com/doc/workbench/en/wb-tables-physical-schemata.html, MySQL

Figure 'table_name': It removes only the figure associated with the table.

At the same time, if the table editor is not open, the Edit 'table_name' item opens it. If it is already activated, the selected table replaces the previous one. Edit 'table_name' in New Tab opens an additional table editor tab. Any tables added to the Physical Schemas section also show up in the Catalog Tree palette within the EER Diagram tab. They may be included in an EER Diagram by dragging and dropping them from this palette.

Tables can also be inserted into an EER Diagram using the table tool on the vertical toolbar. For that, make sure that the EER Diagram tab is selected, then right-click the table icon on the vertical toolbar. Clicking the mouse on this icon changes the mouse pointer to a table pointer. You can also change the mouse pointer to a table pointer by pressing the T key.

Selecting the table tool changes the contents of the toolbar that displays immediately below the menu bar. When the Tables pointer is active, this toolbar presents a schemas list, an engines list, a collations list, and a color chart list. Make use of these lists to select the appropriate schema, engine, collation, and color accent for the new table. You need to associate the new table with a database so that engine and collation of a table can be modified using the table editor. The color of your table can be changed using the Properties palette. The Default Engine and Default Collation values refer to the database defaults.

On the other hand, creating a table by clicking anywhere on the EER Diagram canvas creates a new table with the default name table1. And if you want to revert to the default mouse pointer, click the arrow icon at the top of the vertical toolbar. The Primary Key is indicated by a key icon and indexed fields are indicated by a different colored diamond icon. Click the arrow to the right of the table name to call upon the display of the fields. You can get the display of indexes and triggers in the same way.

Right-clicking a table opens a pop-up menu with the following items:[2]

```
Cut 'table_name'
Copy 'table_name'
Paste
Edit 'table_name'
Edit 'table_name' in New Tab…
Copy SQL to Clipboard
Copy Column Names to Clipboard
Copy Inserts to Clipboard
Copy Insert Template to Clipboard
Delete 'table_name'
Remove Figure 'table_name'
```

When creating the schema for a database, one of the SQL sub-languages, Data Definition Language (DDL) is engaged to do this. However, there are other parts of a database's schema that are controlled and administered by another of SQL's sub-language, Data Control Language (DCL).

DCL is mainly concerned with checking who is permitted to perform certain actions within a database, or, to

---

[2] https://dev.mysql.com/doc/workbench/en/wb-using-table-tool.html, MySQL

put it simply, with the "security of a database." Although we will not look at DCL in detail in this book, it is worth understanding that the "security settings" defined by DCL are also part of the database's operational system. We can see an indication of this if we look closely at the information returned by the \dt meta-command. When we apply \dt, we see a table of information, schema, name, type, and owner. And all of these items of the database's schema could be used by DCL to allow or limit access to certain parts of the database or specific tables. The value in the owner column, in particular, is very much a DCL task; for instance, you could add a restriction to a table so that other users can add, read, update, and delete data from the table but only the owner can modify the structure of the table or cut out the table entirely. You can perceive this in terms of different users having different levels of permission to the database.

To recap the ground we have covered so far:

- Tables are created using the CREATE TABLE SQL command.

- Table column definitions go between the parentheses of the table creation statement.

- Table column definitions consist of a column name, a data type, and optional constraints.

- There are many different data types.

- Although database schema is largely a DDL concern, parts of it, such as access and permissions, are defined by DCL.

The majority of databases you will have to work with as a developer will have more than one table, and those tables will be interrelated with each other in various ways to form table relationships. It is therefore important to explore the reasons for having multiple tables in a database, look at how to define relationships between different tables, and profile the different types of table relationships that can exist.

It is easier to think of a diagram as a simple Entity Relationship Diagram (ERD). An ERD is a graphical depiction of entities and their relationships to each other and is a commonly applied tool within database modeling.

There are different types of ERD starting from conceptual to extremely detailed, and often using specific descriptions such as foot notation to model relationships. We shall not go into the details of these different types, for now, it is simply useful to think of an ERD as any diagram which frames relationships between entities.

Once we have outlined that there are certain relationships existing between tables in ERD, we can actually start to implement those relationships in terms of table schema using keys. Here keys stand for are a special type of constraint utilized to establish relationships and highlight their uniqueness. They can be used to point to a specific row in the current table or to refer to a specific row in another table. Let us look at two types of keys that bring about these particular roles: Primary Keys and Foreign Keys.

## Primary Keys

A requisite part of establishing relationships between two entities or two parts of data is being able to certify the data correctly. Particularly in MySQL, uniquely recognizing data is crucial. A Primary Key is a unique identifier for a row of data.

In order to function as a unique identifier, a column should hold some data, and that data should be unique to each row. In fact, making a column a PRIMARY KEY is essentially similar to attaching NOT NULL and UNIQUE constraints to that column. However, even if any column in a table can have UNIQUE and NOT NULL constraints applied to them, each table can have only one Primary Key. It is common practice for that Primary Key to be a column named id. And while a column of any name can act as the Primary Key, using a column named id is advantageous for collective reasons and so is a popular option.

Being able to clearly identify a row of data in a table via that table's Primary Key column is only half the procedure needed to create relationships between tables. The other half would be to learn how to activate the Primary Key's partner, the Foreign Key.

## Foreign Keys

A Foreign Key enables us to link and associate a row in one table to a row in another table. This is achieved by setting a column in one table as a Foreign Key and having that column reference another table's Primary Key column. Creating this relationship is possible through using the REFERENCES keyword in this form: FOREIGN KEY (fk_col_name) REFERENCES target_table_name (pk_col_name); In general terms, you can think of this reference as establishing a connection between rows in different tables. It is best to try and look through an example.

For instance, you have two tables; one is designated for colors and the other one for shapes. The color_id column of the shapes table is a Foreign Key which references the id column of the colors table. Let us imagine that the "Red" row of our colors table is associated with the "Square" and "Star" rows of the shapes table. Similarly, "Blue" is connected to "Triangle" and "Green" with "Circle." "Orange" would not be associated with any row in the shapes table, but might be potentially available to creating such an association if we add another row into shapes with a color_id of 3.

By setting up this reference, you are securing the referential balance of a relationship. Referential balance is the guarantee that a column value within a record gets a reference of the same existing value; if it does not match, then an error occurs. Namely, MySQL will not let you add a value to the Foreign Key column of a table if the Primary Key column of the table it is referencing does not actually hold that value.

Another way in which a Foreign Key is applied as part of a table's schema depends on the type of relationship you want to set between tables. In order to execute that schema correctly, it is practical to formally describe the relationships you need to model between those entities. As in, you want to define your constraints in the following manner first, before actually acting upon any keys operation:

- A User can have ONE house. A house can have only ONE user OR.

- A User can have MANY houses that he/she may have checked in or lived in. A house can be/ have been checked in by MANY users.

The entity relationships described above can be classified into three relationship types:

- **one-to-one:** A one-to-one relationship between two entities exists when a particular entity item is placed in one table, and it can have only one associated entity in another table. To illustrate: A user can have only one house, and a house belongs to only one user. This example is contrived: in the real world, users can have multiple houses, and multiple people can live in the same house. Yet in the database frame, this type of arrangement is implemented in the following manner: the id that is the PRIMARY KEY of the user's table is used as both the FOREIGN KEY and PRIMARY KEY of the houses table.

- **one-to-many:** A one-to-many relationship exists between two entities if an entity item in one of the tables can be connected to multiple records (entity occurrences) in the other table. The opposite relationship does not exist; that is, each entity occurrence in the second table can only be connected to one entity instance in the first table. For instance, a review is associated with only one book. A book can have many reviews.

- **many-to-many:** A many-to-many relationship is possible between two entities if for one entity occurrence there may be multiple records in the other table and vice versa. For example, a user can check into many houses. A house can be checked in by many users (over an extended period of time). However, in order to execute this type of relationship we need to introduce a third, cross-reference table. This table would hold the relationship between the two entities, by having two FOREIGN KEYs, each of which references the PRIMARY KEY of one of the tables for which you need to create this relationship.

Adding Foreign Key relationships using an EER Diagram is quite straightforward. You can choose from six Foreign Key tools at the vertical toolbar on the left side of an EER Diagram:

- one-to-one non-identifying relationship
- one-to-many non-identifying relationship
- one-to-one identifying relationship
- one-to-many identifying relationship
- many-to-many identifying relationship
- Place a relationship using existing columns

Significant dissimilarities include the following:

- **An identifying relationship: identified by a solid line between tables:** An identifying relationship is one where the child table cannot be uniquely described without its parent. This usually occurs where an intermediary table is brought to resolve a many-to-many relationship. In such instances, the Primary Key is usually a collective key made up of the Primary Keys from the two original tables.

- **A non-identifying relationship: identified by a bro-ken (or dashed) line between tables:** You can create or drag and drop the tables that you want connected to ensure that there is a Primary Key in the table that stays as "one" side of the relationship. Next, you have to click on the appropriate tool for the type of relation-ship you wish to establish. If you are creating a one-to-many relationship, first click the table that is on the "many" side of the relationship, then on the table hold-ing the referenced key. This creates a column in the table on the many sides of the relationship. The default name of this column is table_name_key_name where the table name and the key name both address to the table carrying the referenced key.

When the many-to-many tool is action, double-clicking a table makes an associative table with a many-to-many relationship. However, for this tool to work, there must be a Primary Key placed in the initial table. To edit the characteristics of a Foreign Key, double-click anywhere on the connection line that associates the two tables. This will open the relationship editor.

Pausing your mouse pointer over a relationship connec-tor will highlight the connector, its caption, and the related keys. If the placement of a connection's caption is not suit-able, you can change its position by dragging it to a dif-ferent location. In case you have set a secondary caption, its position can also be changed. You can select multiple connections by holding down the Control key as you click a connection. This can be particularly handy for highlight-ing specific relationships on an EER diagram.

## The Relationship Editor

Double-clicking a relationship on the EER diagram platform activates the relationship editor that primarily has two tabs: Relationship and Foreign Key.

In the Relationship tab, you can set the caption of a relationship using the Caption field that is displayed on the canvas. The default value for this name is fk_source_table_destination_table. You can use the Model menu, Menu Options menu item to out a project-specific default name for Foreign Keys.

The Visibility Settings section is used to define how the relationship is displayed on the EER Diagram canvas. Fully Visible is the default but you can also select to hide relationship lines or to use split lines. Here, a broken line connector indicates a non-identifying relationship. The split line style can be used with an identifying relationship or a non-identifying relationship. It is used for presentation purposes only and does not specify anything about the nature of a relationship.

## Foreign Key Tab

The Foreign Key tab has several sections: Referencing Table, Cardinality, and Referenced Table. The obligatory checkboxes are used to choose whether the referencing table and the referenced table are mandatory. By default, both of these constraints applied (indicated by the checkboxes being checked).

The Cardinality section has a set of radio buttons that let you choose whether the relationship is one-to-one or one-to-many. There is also a check box that enables you to indicate whether the relationship is an identifying relationship or not.

You should right-click a connection to select its properties. Thus, when a connection is selected, it is highlighted, and its properties are presented in the properties canvas. Connection properties are different from the properties of other objects. The following list describes them:[3]

- **caption:** The name of the connection. By default, the name is the name of the Foreign Key and the property is centered above the connection line.

- **captionXOffs:** The X offset of the caption.

- **captionYOffs:** The Y offset of the caption.

- **comment:** The comment associated with the relationship.

- **drawSplit:** Whether to show the relationship as a continuous line.

- **endCaptionXOffs:** The X termination point of the caption offset.

- **endCaptionYOffs:** The Y termination point of the caption offset.

- **extraCaption:** A secondary caption. By default, this extra caption is centered beneath the connection line.

- **extraCaptionXOffs:** The X offset of the secondary caption.

- **extraCaptionYOffs:** The Y offset of the secondary caption.

---

[3] https://dev.mysql.com/doc/workbench/en/wb-connection-properties.html, MySQL

- **mandatory:** Whether the entities are mandatory.

- **many:** False if the relationship is a one-to-one relationship.

- **middleSegmentOffset:** The offset of the middle section of the connector.

- **modelOnly:** Set when the connection will not be propagated to the DDL. It is just a logical connection drawn on a diagram. This is used, for example, when drawing tables with a visual relationship, but with no Foreign Keys.

- **name:** The name used to identify the connection on the EER Diagram canvas. Note that this is not the name of the Foreign Key.

- **referredMandatory:** Whether the referred entity is mandatory.

- **startCaptionXOffs:** The start of the X offset of the caption.

- **startCaptionYOffs:** The start of the Y offset of the caption.

In most cases, you can change the properties of a relationship using the relationship editor and not the Properties canvas.

If you make a relationship invisible by storing it away using the relationship editor's Visibility Settings, and then close the relationship editor, you will not be able to select the relationship to call up its relationship editor. In order to make the relationship visible again, you should expand the table object relating to the relationship in the Layers canvas and choose the relationship object. To edit the selected object, right-click it, then select Edit Object. You can then change the Visibility Settings to Fully Visible so it could appear in the EER Diagram window.

At this point, it is also important to discuss a topic that is essential when dealing with table relationships: referential integrity. This is a concept used when discussing relational data which states that table relationships must always be consistent. Different databases might be able to apply referential integrity rules differently, but the concept has to stay the same.

The constraints we have defined for the user and houses example above enforces the one-to-one relationship, whereby a user can only have one address and an address must have one, and only one, the user. This is a typical example of referential integrity. To demonstrate how it works:

What happens if we try to add another house to a user who already has one?

```
INSERT INTO houses (user_id, street, city,
state)
VALUES (1, '2 Park Avenue', 'NY', 'USA');
Copy Code
ERROR: duplicate key value violates unique
constraint "houses_pkey"
DETAIL: Key (user_id)=(1) already exists.
```

The error above occurs because we are trying to insert a value 1 into the user_id column when such a value already exists in that column. The UNIQUE constraint on the column does not let us do so.

How about if we try to add a house for a user who does not exist?

```
INSERT INTO houses (user_id, street, city,
state) VALUES
(7, '11 Station Avenue', 'Portland', 'USA');
Copy Code
ERROR: insert or update on table
"addresses" violates Foreign Key constraint
"houses_user_id_fkey"
DETAIL: Key (user_id)=(7) is not present
in table "users".
```

Here, we get a different error. The FOREIGN KEY constraint on the user_id column prevents us from adding the value 7 to that column because that value is not present in the id column of the user's table.

In this case, if you are wondering why you can add a user without an address but cannot add an address without a user, this is due to the modality of the relationship between the two entities. There is no need to know exactly what this means for now, but it is important to be aware of this aspect of entity relationships.

## The ON DELETE Clause

Once you get to it, you might also be able to notice in the table creation statement for the houses table, the FOREIGN KEY definition included a clause that read ON DELETE CASCADE. Including this clause, and setting it to CASCADE basically means that if the row being referenced is removed, the row referencing it also disappears. There are alternatives to CASCADE such as SET NULL or SET DEFAULT, which, instead of removing the referencing row will set a new value in the suitable column for that row.

Deciding what to do in cases where you delete a row that is referenced by another row is a significant design decision and is part of the concept of monitoring referential integrity. If you do not put such clauses, you basically leave the decision of what to do up to the database. In the case of MySQL, if you remove a row that is being referenced by a row in another table and you have no ON DELETE clause for that reference, then an error will occur.

## STORING ROUTINES

A stored routine is a named package of SQL statements that are located on the server. There is no need for users to keep re-issuing the individual statements when they can refer to the stored routine instead.

Stored routine types:

- **Stored procedures:** Invoke procedures with a CALL statement. They can pass back values using output variables or result sets.

- **Stored functions:** Call functions inside a statement that return scalar values.

While both types of routines hold SQL statements, MySQL has several key limitations on stored functions that are not suitable for stored procedures, as follows:[4]

- Stored functions cannot use SQL statements that return result sets.

- Stored functions cannot use SQL statements that perform transactional commits or rollbacks.

- Stored functions cannot call themselves recursively.

- Stored functions must produce a return value.

Setting MySQL statements into server-side routines has four important advantages:

1. A stored routine is located on the database server, rather than in the application. For applications based on a client-server structure, calling a stored routine is more convenient and requires less network interaction than transmitting an entire complex of

---

[4] https://dev.mysql.com/doc/workbench/en/wb-routines.html, MySQL

SQL statements and making decisions on the result menu. Stored routines also reduce code repetition by letting developers take out commonly used SQL operations into a single occurrence. The final result is smaller, more systematic, and easier to read application code.

2. A stored routine is made once but used many times, usually from more than one program. If the routine changes, the changes are completed in one spot (the routine definition) while the routine references remain unchanged. This fact can make code maintenance and upgrade much simpler. In addition, as errors can be traced and fixed with minimal impact to the application code, debugging and testing an application also becomes easier.

3. Implementing database operations as stored routines can also affect application security because application modules can be refused access to certain tables and only granted access to the routines that operate those tables. This not only guarantees that an application only uses the data it needs but also ensures reliable implementation of specific tasks or subtasks across the application.

4. Managing stored routines requires abstract thinking because packaging SQL operations into a stored routine are similar to understanding how a specific task may be compressed into a generic component. With that, using stored routines encourages the creation of a more efficient and versatile application structure.

You can add Routine Groups to a database either from the Physical Schemata section of the MySQL Model page or from an EER Diagram. While routines may be added only from the Physical Schemata section of the MySQL Model page.

If you want to view an existing schema together with its Routines and Routine Groups, choose Database and Reverse Engineer from the main menu. After the schema has been included in the current model, you can see the schema items on the Physical Schemata platform on the MySQL Model page. The Routines and Routine Groups will all be listed there.

MySQL Workbench unites both stored procedures and stored functions into one logical item called a Routine. Routine Groups are used to assemble related routines. You can define Routine with the Routine Group Editor to assign specific routines to a group, using a drag and drop function. When designing an EER Diagram, you can place the Routine Groups on the main platform by dragging them straight from the Catalog Palette. However, placing single routines on the diagram is not possible, as it would clutter the space.

## Adding Routines to the Physical Schemata

In order to add a routine, double-click the Add Routine icon in the Physical Schemata section of the MySQL Model page. The default name of the routine is routine1. In case a routine with this name already exists, the new routine will automatically be named routine2. Adding a new routine opens the routine editor located at the bottom of the application. Right-clicking a routine opens a pop-up menu with the following items:

- Rename

- Cut 'routine_name'

- Copy 'routine_name'

- Paste

- Edit Routine

- Edit in New Window

- Copy SQL to Clipboard

- Delete 'routine_name'

To be precise, the Edit Routine item opens the routine editor. While the cut and paste items are of great use when copying routines between different schemata.

It is also important to keep in mind that deleting the code for a routine from the Routines tab of the Routine Group Editor results in the removal of the whole routine item from the model. To remove a routine from a routine group, you need to use the controls on the Routine Group tab of the Routine Group Editor. The action of the delete option differs depending upon how you have modified MySQL Workbench.

To call upon the routine editor, double-click a routine in the Physical Schemata section on the MySQL Model page. This opens the routine editor placed at the bottom of the application. Any number of routines may be operating at the same time with each additional routine appearing as a tab at the top of the routine editor. Yet Routine and

Privileges tabs appear at the bottom of the routine editor. You can navigate between different tabs using the mouse or from the keyboard by pressing Control+Alt+Tab.

### The Routine Tab

You can use the Routine tab of the routine editor to accomplish the following tasks:

- Renaming the routine using the Name field

- Entering the SQL to create a routine using the SQL field

### The Privileges Tab

The Privileges tab of the routine editor lets you assign specific roles and privileges. You can also assign privileges to a role using the role editor. When this tab is first activated, all roles that have been made are listed on the right. Move the roles you wish to connect with this table to the Roles list on the left. You can do this by picking a role and then clicking the < button. Use the Shift key to select multiple contiguous roles and the Control key to choosing noncontiguous roles.

To assign privileges to a role, click the role in the Roles list. This presents all available privileges in the Assigned Privileges list. The list of privileges listed typically includes the following:

- ALL

- CREATE

- DROP

- GRANT OPTION

- REFERENCES

- ALTER

- DELETE

- INDEX

- INSERT

- SELECT

- UPDATE

- TRIGGER

You can assign all privileges to a particular role or any other privilege as listed above. Privileges unrelated to a table, such as the FILE privilege, will not be displayed. If a role has already been assigned privileges on a specific table, those privileges show as already checked in the Assigned Privileges list.

## Adding Routine Groups to the Physical Schemata

Double-clicking the Add Routine Group icon in the Physical Schemata section of the MySQL Model page includes a routine group with the default name of routines1. If a routine group with this name already exists, the new routine group will be named routines2.

Adding a new routine group automatically opens the routine group's editor located at the bottom of the application. Right-clicking a routine group activates a pop-up menu with the following items:

- Rename

- Cut 'routine_group_name'

- Copy 'routine_group_name'

- Edit Routine

- Edit in New Window

- Copy SQL to Clipboard

- Delete 'routine_group_name'

Here, the cut and paste items are useful for copying routine groups between different schemata. Deleting a routine group from the MySQL Model page removes the group but does not remove any routines holding in that group.

Any routine groups included in the Physical Schemata also pop up in the Catalog platform on the right side of the application. They may be attached to an EER diagram by dragging and dropping them from this platform.

### Adding Routine Groups to an EER Diagram

In order to add routine groups to an EER Diagram, you can use the Routine Groups tool that is on the vertical toolbar. Make sure that the EER Diagram tab is selected, then right-click the routine group's icon on the vertical toolbar that is situated right above the lowest toolbar separator. Clicking the mouse on this icon will transform the mouse pointer into a routine group pointer. You can also change the mouse pointer to a routine pointer by pressing the G key.

Choosing the Routine Group tool changes the contents of the toolbar that appears immediately below the menu bar. When the Routine Groups pointer is operating, this toolbar holds a schemata list and a color chart list. It is possible to use these lists to select the appropriate schema and color palette for the new routine group. The color of your routine group can later be changed through the Properties palette. At the same time, you need to make sure that you associate the new routine group with a database.

Additionally, you can also create a routine group by clicking anywhere on the EER Diagram canvas. This creates a new routine group with the default name routines1. To return back to the default mouse pointer, just click the arrow icon at the top of the vertical toolbar. Right-clicking a routine group opens a pop-up menu, and even though there is no rename option, the behavior of the delete option can be determined by your MySQL Workbench Options Settings.

## Modifying a Routine Group Using the Properties Palette

To call upon the routine group editor, double-click a routine group object on the EER Diagram platform or double-click a routine group in the Physical Schemata part on the MySQL Model page. This activates the routine group editor placed at the bottom of the application. Double-clicking the title bar displays the editor fully but doing the same can also hide it. As already mentioned, you can have any number of routine groups open at the same time, with every additional routine group appearing as a tab at the top of the routine editor.

Similar to other groups, Routine group, and Privileges tabs appear at the bottom of the routine editor, and you can navigate between them using the mouse or from the keyboard by pressing Control+Alt+Tab.

## The Routine Groups Tab

The Routine Groups tab of the routine group's editor is perfect to get the following tasks done:[5]

- Renaming the routine group using the Name field

- Adding routines to the group by dragging and dropping them

- Adding comments to the routine group

Stored routines can be particularly beneficial in certain situations such as:

If multiple client applications are written in different languages or operate on different platforms, but require the same database operations to perform. Or when security is of the utmost importance, you can use stored procedures and functions for all regular operations. This provides some sense of stability and security, knowing that all routines can each operation are properly logged. In such an environment, applications and users would have no access to the database tables directly but can only administer specific stored routines.

Thus, stored routines can provide better quality performance because less information needs to be transferred between the server and the client. At the same time, this does increase the load on the database server due to the fact that most of the work is done on the server-side and less is done on the client-side.

---

[5] https://dev.mysql.com/doc/workbench/en/wb-routines.html#wb-routine-editor, MySQL

Stored routines also let you have libraries of functions located in the database server. This is a feature shared by modern applications that ensure that such design is available internally. So that using these client application language features is beneficial even for the developer outside the scope of database use.

## Stored Routine Syntax

A stored routine is either a procedure or a function that is created with the CREATE PROCEDURE or CREATE FUNCTION statements. But if a procedure is invoked using a CALL statement, and can only deliver values using output variables, a function can be called from inside a statement similar to any other function, and can also return a scalar value. The body of a stored routine can use compound statements and might be dropped with the DROP PROCEDURE and DROP FUNCTION statements. In case if you need some alteration you can apply ALTER PROCEDURE and ALTER FUNCTION statements.

A stored procedure or function is typically connected with a particular database. This has several implications:

When the routine is called up, an implicit USE db_name is activated. USE statements within stored routines are not allowed, but you can qualify routine names with the database name. This can be applied when referring to a routine that is not in the current database. For instance, to invoke a stored procedure p or function f that is associated with the test database, you can add CALL test.p or test.f. In addition, when a database is dropped, all stored routines associated with it will be dropped as well as stored functions cannot be recursive.

To be precise, recursion in stored procedures is technically permitted but disabled by default. If you need recursion enables, set the max_sp_recursion_depth server system variable to a value greater than zero. Stored procedure recursion increases the demand for thread stack space. If you increase the value of max_sp_recursion_depth, you might need to increase thread stack size by increasing the value of thread_stack at server startup.

MySQL holds up a very useful extension that enables the use of regular SELECT statements inside a stored procedure. The result set of such a query is normally sent directly to the client. Multiple SELECT statements make up multiple result sets, so the client is expected to use a MySQL client library that can bear multiple result sets. This also means that the user should have a client library from a version of MySQL at least as recent as 4.0. and should be able to specify the CLIENT_MULTI_RESULTS option when it connects.

In MySQL 8.0., a user variable referenced by a statement in a stored procedure has its typeset on the first time the procedure is invoked and keeps this type each time the procedure is invoked thereafter.

## Stored Routines and MySQL Privileges

The MySQL grant system takes stored routines into consideration in the following manner:

- The CREATE ROUTINE privilege is typically applied to create stored routines.

- The ALTER ROUTINE privilege is used to advance or drop stored routines. This privilege is granted automatically to the creator of a routine if required and dropped from the creator when the routine is dropped.

- The EXECUTE privilege is necessary to operate stored routines. In addition, you can also administer the default SQL SECURITY characteristic which enables users who have access to the database with which the routine is associated to run it.

However, in case the automatic_sp_privileges system variable is set at 0, the EXECUTE and ALTER ROUTINE privileges are not automatically permitted but rather dropped from the routine creator altogether.

The creator of a routine here stands for the account used to execute the CREATE statement for it. This might not be the same as the account named as the DEFINER in the routine definition that can see all routine properties, including its definition. The creator of a routine account has full access to the routine output as generated by:[6]

- The contents of the INFORMATION_SCHEMA. ROUTINES table

- The SHOW CREATE FUNCTION and SHOW CREATE PROCEDURE statements

- The SHOW FUNCTION CODE and SHOW PROCEDURE CODE statements

- The SHOW FUNCTION STATUS and SHOW PROCEDURE STATUS statements

---

[6] https://dev.mysql.com/doc/workbench/en/wb-routines.html#wb-routine-editor-privileges, MySQL

For an account other than the account named as the routine DEFINER, access to routine items depends on the privileges possessed by the account:

- With the SHOW_ROUTINE privilege or the global SELECT privilege, the account can view all routine properties, including its definition.

- With the CREATE ROUTINE, ALTER ROUTINE or EXECUTE privilege granted at a scope that includes the routine, the account can view all routine properties except its definition.

Stored Routine Metadata

In order to acquire metadata about stored routines, you can follow this regulation:[7]

- Query the ROUTINES table of the INFORMATION_ SCHEMA database

- Use the SHOW CREATE PROCEDURE and SHOW CREATE FUNCTION statements to view routine definitions

- Use the SHOW PROCEDURE STATUS and SHOW FUNCTION STATUS statements to review routine characteristics

- Use the SHOW PROCEDURE CODE and SHOW FUNCTION CODE statements to see a representation of the internal operation of the routine

---

[7] https://dev.mysql.com/doc/workbench/en/wb-routines.html#wb-routine-editor-privileges, My SQL

*Stored Procedures, Functions, Triggers,*
*and LAST_INSERT_ID*

Within the body of a stored routine (procedure or function) or a trigger, the value of LAST_INSERT_ID changes the same way as for statements implemented outside the body of these items. The effect of a stored routine or trigger upon the value of LAST_INSERT_ID that is seen by the following statements depends on the type of routine:

If a stored procedure applies statements that transform the value of LAST_INSERT_ID, the modified value is seen by statements that follow the procedure call. Yet for stored functions and triggers that change the value, the value is restored when the function or trigger ends, so the following statements do not see a changed value.

## REVERSE ENGINEERING A DATABASE

There are at times cases where you can have a relational database schema implemented, but it certainly lacks the original Relational or Entity-Relationship (ER) models that were used to design the database. Nevertheless, you may be able to re-create the ER model by reverse-engineering the model from the database system. The process of building a physical database from the ER diagram is called forward engineering. Yet sometimes when you need to do the opposite—namely, create a diagram from existing database schema you would be looking at the task that is called reverse engineering. To achieve such a task, you would need to take the following steps:

- Firstly, to connect the database schema and identify all of the existing tables, their columns as well as Primary and Foreign Key constraints

- Next, to structure the Relational Model that is connected to the existing set of tables and constraints

- And at last, to recollect the ER model from the relational model

As a prerequisite, you supposed to have downloaded and installed MySQL Workbench. You will also need the credentials (hostname, port, service name, username, and password) to insert into the sample MySQL database schema. With MySQL Workbench, you can reverse-engineer a database using a MySQL create script, or you can connect to a live MySQL server and import a single database or a number of databases.

"To Reverse-Engineer a Database Using a Create Script," follow this guideline:

On the home screen, select the model view from the sidebar, click (>) next to Models, and then click Reverse Engineer MySQL Create Script. With a model selected and its model tab open, click File, Import, and then Reverse Engineer MySQL Create Script from the menu.

With that, tables, views, routines, routine groups, indexes, keys, and constraints would be imported from an SQL script file. Objects imported using an SQL script can be modified within MySQL Workbench in the same way as other items.

However, importing a large number (more than 1000) objects could fail to create an ER diagram and instead launch a resource warning with the text "Too many objects are selected for auto-placement. Select fewer elements to create the ER diagram." In this case, you should activate the reverse engineering wizard by manually creating the

ER diagram, and then importing your numerous objects using the ER diagram catalog viewer.

If your script creates a database, MySQL Workbench generates a new Physical Schemas section within the open MySQL Model tab. Click Execute to reverse-engineer the SQL script, review its results, and optionally place the objects in a new ER diagram. After that, click Next to view a summary of the results and then Finish to close the wizard. Do not forget to save the schema before exiting MySQL Workbench. Click File and then Save from the menu to save the reverse-engineered database as a MySQL Workbench file with the .mwb extension.

## Creating a DDL Script

You can create a data definition (DDL) script by inserting the mysqldump db_name --no-data > script_file.sql command. Using the -no-data option secures that the script holds only DDL statements. However, if you are working with a script that also contains other than DDL statements, there is no need to remove them beforehand, the script will ignore them automatically.

If you plan to redesign a database within MySQL Workbench and then export the changes, make sure to keep a copy of the original DDL script as you will need it to create an ALTER script.

You can also use the -databases option with mysqldump if you want to create the database as well as all its items. If there is no CREATE DATABASE db_name statement in your script file, you should import the database items into the existing schema or, if there is no schema, a new unnamed schema is created automatically.

"To reverse-engineer a live database," click Database and then select Reverse Engineer from the menu. The first step of the wizard lets you set up a connection to the live database you are going to reverse-engineer. You can set up a new connection or select a previously created stored connection. Usual information needed for the connection includes hostname, user name, and password.

After this information has been inserted, or you have selected a stored connection, click the Next option to go to the next step. Review the displayed information to make sure that the connection did not lead to any errors, then click Next.

The next step presents the schemas available on the server. Select the check box of each schema you wish to process. After you have selected the desired schemas, click the Next button to continue. The wizard then showcases the tasks it took and summarizes the results of the operation. Check the results carefully before clicking Next to continue.

The next step opens the Select Objects to Reverse Engineer page. It has a section for each object type available in the schema that you can import (tables, views, routines, and others). All object types are there by default. The Place imported items on a diagram option is also selected by default.

At the same time, keep in mind that importing 250 or more objects could fail to generate an ER diagram and instead display a resource warning with the text "Too many objects are selected for auto-placement. Select fewer elements to create the ER diagram." In this case, execute the reverse engineering wizard manually, and then import all the objects using the ER diagram catalog viewer.

On the other hand, if you do not wish to import all the objects from the existing database, you have the option of filtering which objects should be imported. Thus, each section has a Show Filter button. Click this button if you do not want to import all the objects of a particular type. After that, you can select which data to import and then hide the filter by clicking Hide Filter. Next, click Execute to continue to the next step.

The wizard then imports objects, displaying the tasks that have been completed and whether the operation was accomplished fully or not. If errors occurred, you can click Show Logs to see the matter of the errors. The next section will show an example of the operational progress, which was completed successfully. Click Next to continue to the final step.

The final step of the wizard displays a summary of the reverse-engineered objects. Click Finish to close the wizard. Before closing MySQL Workbench, make sure to save the schema. Then, click File and Save from the menu to save the reverse-engineered database as a MySQL Workbench file with the .mwb extension.

As a final remark, it is worth noting that during reverse engineering, the application checks for tables and views that duplicate existing names and does not allow that. So in case you try to import an item that duplicates the name of an existing object, you will get an error message. You can see all the errors that have occurred during reverse engineering, through the Show Logs option. Clicking on it will create a panel containing a list of messages, including error messages that may have occurred.

As an alternative, if you plan to import an item with the same name as an existing object, make sure to rename the existing object before reverse engineering. If you transfer objects from more than one schema, there will be a tab in the Physical Schemas area of the MySQL Model page for each schema imported. You cannot reverse-engineer a live database that has the same name as an existing schema. Therefore, in order to reuse a schema name, you must rename the existing schema first. In the next chapter, we shall look into management instances as such that include SQL Scripts and Files in more detail.

# CHAPTER 4

# SQL Development

## IN THIS CHAPTER

➤ Analysing solutions of SQL development

➤ Learning how to run SQL files

➤ Editing SQL different data types more efficiently

DOI: 10.1201/9781003229629-4

More and more businesses today demand great real-time analytics about their enterprise. In response, some companies started to add embedded analytics to their SaaS applications as a way to increase the overall value proposition. Others see it as an opportunity to create additional revenue lines by using their vast stores of data to serve up big data analytics. Naturally, SQL development tools and capacities play a big role in data application development. Yet, at the same time, developers should be selecting the tools in their toolbox carefully to ensure they can create and implement the most effective data applications possible for their internal and external procedures.

New data apps tend to be built almost entirely on public cloud infrastructure and apply the Application Programming Interface to assemble together all the core features. However, not all cloud-based solutions are created equally. Many software developers start their app journey by opting for low-cost tools that allow quick development without upfront investment. For instance, open-source tools such as PostgreSQL, Elasticsearch, and NoSQL databases were popular at the time due to the fact that they propose an easy starting point to get up and start running. This shortcut enables a new analytics app to be sent to market without the upfront cost of procuring a database, which reduces a potential discord between development and finance teams. Nevertheless, such open-source tools, including MySQL are now facing particular development challenges that occur when you do not consider thoroughly what is needed from a data stack to deliver powerful service and analytics:

1. There is a need to increase data storage and compute strains on the system. This request typically comes from larger customers. Now open source solutions still require manual and disruptive scaling that impacts the customer experience and requires more time and effort for engineering.

2. Users observe a lack of native support for semi-structured data as using data types such as JSON, XML, and Avro is a huge challenge, especially when the open-source solution does not natively support semi-structured data. This forces experts to build and maintain complex data pipelines.

3. Maintenance: While development teams should spend their time coding and developing analytics applications, open-source solutions also require frequent upgrades and maintenance. As a result, developers end up spending most of their time and resources dealing with system maintenance instead of what they are supposed to do in the first place—coding.

4. Know-how: The use of open-source tools mostly requires specific skills that may not exist within an organization. As a consequence, companies need to hire more experts, which is typically problematic to find and expensive to attain.

With these very current challenges in mind, the SQL Server development tools have to rush and streamline the application development process. On the other hand, the SQL Server development applications have a rich integrated development environment (IDE), able to provide an opportunity for object re-use, integrate with source control applications like Visual Source Safe, and much more.

## MANAGING SQL SCRIPTS

One of the main developers' activities is to manage SQL scripts and environments for the database. While managing multiple copies, sometimes it requires refreshing from a production environment to the lower environment. For that you need to copy all database objects such as database schema, tables, as well as use multiple approaches such as database backup restore, depending upon the requirement. In this section, we will look closely at how to manage SQL scripts in different ways.

We can use Generate Scripts wizard to script all database objects or specific objects. It provides various configuration options to select from. Start by right-clicking on the source SQL database for which you want to generate script and launch Generate scripts wizard that comes with a brief introduction and activity options to choose from:

- Select database objects
- Specify scripting options
- Review your selections
- Generate scripts and save them
- Generate Scripts Wizard for database objects

Once you click Next, you get options to script an entire database or select specific objects from the following list:

- Tables
- Views
- Stored procedure
- User-defined functions
- User-defined data types
- DDL triggers
- XML schema collections
- Schemas
- Full-text catalogs
- Select objects

Let's imagine you need to script the entire database. Here, you get different options to save the script:

- Script to file
- Script to a new query window
- Script to clipboard
- Advanced configurations

From here, click on Advanced to see what Advanced Scripting Options are available.

Advanced Scripting Options

In this window, you can accomplish the required changes for generating a script for the selected objects. We shall not cover all configurations here, just a few configurations that are set by default:

- **Script drop and create:** Default configuration used to generate script with a Create statement.

- **Script for server version:** Useful configuration in case you need to script for a different version of SQL Server. You can use SQL Server versions starting from SQL Server 2005, but you should generate a script for an appropriate version as few commands and syntaxes do not operate in a different version of SQL Server.

- **Script for the database engine edition:** You can select the required database engine edition, and its script features in tune with that edition.

- **Script logins, object-level permissions, owner, statistics:** By default, you cannot script any of the logins, object-level permissions, database owner, and statistics. You can change the corresponding value to true so that it generates those scripts as well.

- **Type of data to the script:** Is used to script for the selected objects. You can edit this configuration and choose from Data only, Schema and Data and Schema only value.

- **Table/view options:** Provides various configurations for script tables and views such as script constraints, indexes, primary and foreign keys.

Once you have configured the required options, click Next for a review of the selections. You can go back and change any settings. If no changes needed, click Next, and you can see the status for each object script. Once you are done with it, you can see the script per the configured option.

MySQL Server is a single multithreaded program that completes most of the processes in a MySQL installation. It manages access to the MySQL data directory that contains databases and tables. The data directory is also the default location for other information such as log files and status files. And when MySQL server starts, it monitors network connections from client programs and manages access to databases on behalf of those clients. The MySQL program has many options that you can see if you run this command:

```
mysqld -verbose -help
```

MySQL Server also has a set of system variables that impact its operation as it runs. System variables can be arranged at server startup, and many of them can be modified at runtime to effect dynamic server reconfiguration. MySQL Server also has a set of status variables that hold information about its operation. You can observe these status variables to access runtime performance characteristics.

### *mysqld_safe – MySQL Server Startup Script*

mysqld_safe is the recommended way to start a mysqld server on Unix. mysqld_safe has important safety features such as restarting the server when an error occurs and logging runtime information to an error log. For some Linux platforms, MySQL installation from Debian packages includes systemd support for managing MySQL server startup and shutdown. On these platforms, mysqld_safe is not installed because it is not necessary.

mysqld_safe is also a great way to start an executable named mysqld. To override the default behavior and define explicitly the name of the server you need to run, insert a --mysqld or --mysqld-version option to mysqld_safe. You can also use -ledir to state the directory where mysqld_safe should search for the server.

Options unfamiliar to mysqld_safe are passed to mysqld if they are specified on the command line but omitted if they are identified in the [mysqld_safe] group of an option file.

mysqld_safe reads all options from the [mysqld], [server], and [mysqld_safe] sections in option files. To illustrate, if you specify a [mysqld] section like this, mysqld_safe finds and uses the --log-error option:

```
[mysqld]
log-error=error.log
```

For backward consistency, mysqld_safe also reads [safe_mysqld] sections, but to be current you should rename such sections to [mysqld_safe].

mysqld_safe accepts scripts on the command line and in option files, as described:[1]

| Option Name | Description |
| --- | --- |
| basedir | Path to MySQL installation directory |
| core-file-size | Size of core file that mysqld should be able to create |
| datadir | Path to data directory |
| defaults-extra-file | Read named option file in addition to usual option files |
| defaults-file | Read-only named option file |
| help | Display help message and exit |
| ledir | Path to directory where server is located |
| log-error | Write error log to named file |
| malloc-lib | Alternative malloc library to use for mysqld |
| mysqld | Name of server program to start (in ledir directory) |
| mysqld-safe-log-timestamps | Timestamp format for logging |
| mysqld-version | Suffix for server program name |
| nice | Use nice program to set server scheduling priority |
| no-defaults | Read no option files |

*(Continued)*

---

[1]  https://dev.mysql.com/doc/refman/8.0/en/mysqld-safe.html, MySQL

| Option Name | Description |
| --- | --- |
| open-files-limit | Number of files that mysqld should be able to open |
| PID-file | Pathname of server process ID file |
| plugin-dir | Directory where plugins are installed |
| port | Port number on which to listen for TCP/IP connections |
| skip-kill-mysqld | Do not try to kill stray mysqld processes |
| skip-Syslog | Do not write error messages to Syslog; use error log file |
| socket | Socket file on which to listen for Unix socket connections |
| syslog | Write error messages to Syslog |
| syslog-tag | Tag suffix for messages written to Syslog |
| timezone | Set TZ time zone environment variable to named value |
| user | Run mysqld as user_name or numeric user ID |
| help | Display a help message and exit. |

- **basedir=dir_name:** Evokes the path to the MySQL installation directory.

- **core-file-size=size:** Stands for the size of the core file that mysqld should be able to produce.

- **datadir=dir_name:** The path to the data directory.

- **defaults-extra-file=file_name:** Applied to check available file options. If the file does not exist or is otherwise unavailable, the server exits with an error. If file_name is not an absolute pathname, it is interpreted relative to the current directory. This is typically used as the first option on the command line.

- **defaults-file=file_name:** Similar to the previous directory, if the file does not exist or is otherwise inaccessible, the server exits with an error. If file_name is not an absolute pathname, it is interpreted relative to the current directory.

- **ledir=dir_name:** If mysqld_safe cannot find the server, you can use this option to indicate the pathname to the directory where the server is located. This option is supported only on the command line, not in option files. On platforms that use systemd, the value can be specified in the value of MYSQLD_OPTS.

- **log-error=file_name:** Used to write the error log to the given file.

- **mysqld-safe-log-timestamps:** This option administers the format for timestamps in log output produced by mysqld_safe. The following list describes the allowed values. For any other value, mysqld_safe issues a warning and uses UTC format.[2]

  UTC, UTC
    ISO 8601 UTC format (same as --log_timestamps=UTC for the server). This is the default.

  SYSTEM, system
    ISO 8601 local time format (same as --log_timestamps=SYSTEM for the server).

---

[2] https://dev.mysql.com/doc/refman/8.0/en/mysqld-safe.html, MySQL

HYPHEN, hyphen
YY-MM-DD h:mm:ss format, as in mysqld_safe
for MySQL 5.6.

LEGACY, legacy
YYMMDD hh:mm:ss format, as in mysqld_safe
prior to MySQL 5.6.

- **malloc-lib=[lib_name]**: The name of the library that
is used for memory allocation instead of the system
malloc() library. The option value must be one of the
directories/usr/lib, /usr/lib64, /usr/lib/i386-linux-
gnu, or/usr/lib/x86_64-linux-gnu.

   The --malloc-lib option works by modifying the
LD_PRELOAD environment value to impact linking and enable the memory-allocation library. If the
option is given as --malloc-lib=/path/to/some/library,
that full path should be added to the beginning of the
LD_PRELOAD value. If the full path points to a nonexistent or unavailable file, mysqld_safe strikes with
an error. For cases where mysqld_safe includes a pathname to LD_PRELOAD, it adds the path to the beginning of any existing value the variable already has.

- **mysqld=prog_name**: It stands for the name of the
server program that you need to start. This option is
applied if you use the MySQL binary distribution but
hold the data directory outside of the binary distribution. If mysqld_safe cannot find the server, use the
-ledir option to look for the pathname to the directory where the server is placed. However, this option
can be accepted only on the command line, not in

option files. In systems that use systemd, the value can be specified in the value of MYSQLD_OPTS.

- **mysqld-version=suffix:** This option is similar to the --mysqld option, but you have to define only the suffix for the server program name. The basename is automatically assigned to be mysqld. For instance, if you use --mysqld-version=debug, mysqld_safe starts the mysqld-debug program in the ledir directory. If the argument to --mysqld-version is empty, mysqld_safe uses mysqld in the ledir directory. However, this option can be accepted only on the command line, not in option files. In systems that use systemd, the value can be specified in the value of MYSQLD_OPTS.

- **nice=priority:** Use the nice program to prop the server's scheduling priority to a particular value.

- **no-defaults:** Used to enable reading of any option files. If program startup fails because it was reading unknown options from an option file, --no-defaults can be used to prevent them from being read. This must be the first option on the command line if it is applied.

- **open-files-limit=count:** Stands for the number of files that mysqld should be able to open.

- **pid-file=file_name:** The pathname that mysqld should use to process the ID file.

- **plugin-dir=dir_name:** The standard path name of the plugin directory.

- **port=port_num:** The port number that the server should use when monitoring Transmission Control Protocol/Internet Protocol (TCP/IP) connections. The port number must be 1024 or higher unless the server is started by the root operating system user.

- **skip-kill-mysqld:** Do not try to kill stray mysqld processes at startup. This option operates only for Linux.

- **socket=path:** The Unix socket file that the server should utilize when administering local connections.

- **syslog/-skip-Syslog:** --syslog causes error messages to be sent to Syslog on systems that support the logger program. --skip-Syslog cancels the use of Syslog; messages are written to an error log file. So that when Syslog is used for error logging, the daemon.err facility is used for all log messages.

- **syslog-tag=tag:** For connecting to Syslog, messages from mysqld_safe and mysqld are written with identifiers of mysqld_safe and mysqld. To specify a suffix for the identifiers, use --Syslog-tag=tag, which modifies the identifiers to be mysqld_safe-tag and mysqld-tag.

- **timezone=timezone:** Used to set particular time zone environment variable to the given option value. You should consult your operating system documentation for available time zone specification formats.

- **user={user_name|user_id}:** Used to run the mysqld server as the user having the name user_name or the numeric user ID user_id.

If you implement mysqld_safe with the --defaults-file or --defaults-extra-file option to name an option file, the option must be the first one placed on the command line. For instance, this command does not use the named option file:

```
mysql> mysqld_safe --port=port_num
--defaults-file=file_name
```

Instead, use the following command:

```
mysql> mysqld_safe --defaults-file=file_name
--port=port_num
```

The mysqld_safe script is written so that it typically can start a server that was installed from the binary distribution of MySQL, even though these types of distributions usually install the server in different places. mysqld_safe counts on one of the following conditions to be true:

The server and databases can supposedly be found relative to the working directory. For binary distributions, mysqld_safe looks under its working directory for bin and data directories. For source distributions, it searches for libexec and var directories. This condition should be met if you run mysqld_safe from your MySQL installation directory (for instance, /usr/local/MySQL for a binary distribution).

If the server and databases cannot be found relative to the working directory, mysqld_safe tries to locate them through path names. Typical locations are /usr/local/ libexec and /usr/local/var. The actual locations are defined by the values configured into the distribution at the time it was structured. They should be correct if

MySQL is installed in the location identified at the configuration instance.

Because mysqld_safe tries to look for the server and databases relative to its own working directory, you can install a binary distribution of MySQL anywhere, as long as you execute mysqld_safe from the MySQL installation directory:

```
cd mysql_installation_directory
bin/mysqld_safe &
```

If mysqld_safe fails, even when called upon from the MySQL installation directory, include the --ledir and --datadir options to indicate the directories in which the server and databases are placed on your system.

mysqld_safe tries to apply the sleep and date system utilities to decide how many times per second it has tried to start. If these utilities are present and the attempted starts per second are more than five, mysqld_safe waits 1 full second before starting again. This is made to prevent excessive central processing unit usage in the sequence of repeated failures.

If you use mysqld_safe to start mysqld, mysqld_safe arranges for error messages to occur from itself and from mysqld to go to the same destination. There are a few mysqld_safe options for directing the destination of these messages:

- **log-error=file_name:** Used to generate error messages to the named error file.

- **syslog:** Used to write error messages to Syslog on systems that support the logger program.

- **skip-Syslog:** Used to write a message to the default error log file or to a named file if the --log-error option is given. In case none of these options is given, the default is --skip-Syslog.

### MySQL.server—MySQL Server Startup Script

MySQL distributions on Unix and Unix-like systems include a script named MySQL.server, which starts the MySQL server using mysqld_safe. It is suitable for systems like Linux and Solaris that use System V-style run directories to start and stop system services. It is also used by the macOS Startup Item for MySQL.

MySQL.server is the script name as used within the MySQL source tree. The installed name might be different, but you can adjust the name MySQL.server as appropriate for your system. Also worth noting that for some Linux platforms, MySQL installation from Debian package includes support for managing MySQL server startup and shutdown. On these platforms, MySQL.server and mysqld_safe are not installed because they are not necessary.

To start or stop the server manually using the MySQL.server script, you need to invoke it from the command line with the following start or stop arguments:

- MySQL.server start
- MySQL.server stop

MySQL.server changes location to the MySQL installation directory then invokes mysqld_safe. To run the server as some specific user, add an appropriate user option to the [mysqld] group of the global /etc/my.cnf option file. It is also possible to edit MySQL.server if you have installed a binary distribution of MySQL in a nonstandard location. Modify it to change location into the proper directory before it runs mysqld_safe. Once you do this, your modified version of MySQL.server may be overwritten if you upgrade MySQL, so be sure to make a copy of your edited version that you can reinstall.

To start and stop MySQL automatically on your server, you should add start and stop commands to the appropriate places in your /etc/RC* files. In addition, if you use the Linux server package the MySQL.server script may be installed in the /etc/init.d directory with the name mysqld or MySQL.

If you install MySQL from a source distribution or using a binary distribution format that does not install MySQL. server automatically, you can install the script manually. It can be found in the support-files directory under the MySQL installation directory or in a MySQL source tree. Copy the script to the /etc/init.d directory with the name MySQL and make it executable:

```
cp MySQL.server /etc/init.d/mysql
chmod +x /etc/init.d/mysql
```

After installing the script, the commands needed to activate it to run at system startup depend on your operating system. On Linux, you can use chkconfig:

```
chkconfig --add MySQL
```

On some Linux systems, the following command also seems to be necessary to fully run the MySQL script:

```
chkconfig --level 345 MySQL on
```

On FreeBSD, startup scripts generally go in /usr/local/etc/ rc.d/. Install the mysql.server script as /usr/local/etc/rc.d/ mysql.server.sh to enable automatic startup.

   As an alternative, some operating systems also use /etc/ rc.local or /etc/init.d/boot.local to start additional services on startup. To start up MySQL using this method, apply the following command:

```
/bin/sh -c 'cd /usr/local/mysql;. /bin/
mysqld_safe --user=mysql &'
```

MySQL.server reads options from the [mysql.server] and [mysqld] sections of option files. For backward compatibility, it also reads [mysql_server] sections, but to keep it updated, you should rename such sections to [mysql. server].

   You can also add options for mysql.server in a global /etc/my.cnf file. A typical my.cnf file should look like this:

```
[mysqld]
datadir=/usr/local/mysql/var
socket=/var/tmp/mysql.sock
port=3306
user=mysql
```

The MySQL.server script supports the options shown below. Once specified, they should be placed in an option file, not

on the command line. MySQL.server supports only start
and stop as command-line arguments.[3]

| Option Name | Description |
|---|---|
| basedir | Path to MySQL installation directory |
| datadir | Path to MySQL data directory |
| PID-file | File in which server should write its process ID |
| service-startup-timeout | How long to wait for server startup |

- **basedir=dir_name:** Stands for the path to the MySQL
  installation directory.

- **datadir=dir_name:** Stands for the path to the MySQL
  data directory.

- **pid-file=file_name:** The pathname of the file in
  which the server should insert its process ID. The
  server creates the file in the data directory until an
  absolute pathname is assigned to specify a different
  directory.

  In case this option is not given, MySQL.server
  uses a default value of host_name.pid. The file value
  passed to mysqld_safe overrides any value specified
  in the [mysqld_safe] option filegroup. And because
  MySQL.server reads the [mysqld] option file group
  but not the [mysqld_safe] group, you can ensure
  that mysqld_safe has the same value when called
  from MySQL.server manually by putting the same
  file setting in both the [mysqld_safe] and [mysqld]
  groups.

---

[3] https://dev.mysql.com/doc/refman/8.0/en/mysql-server.html, MySQL

- **service-startup-timeout=seconds:** It is used to indicate how long in seconds you need to wait for confirmation of server startup. If the server does not start within this time, MySQL.server exits with an error. The default value is 900. A value of 0 means you should not wait for startup at all.

*mysqld_multi—Manage Multiple MySQL Servers*
mysqld_multi is designed to run several mysqld processes that monitor connections on different Unix socket files and TCP/IP ports. It can also start or stop servers, as well as report their current status. At the same time, for some Linux platforms, MySQL installation from Debian package includes systemd support for managing MySQL server startup and shutdown. On these platforms, mysqld_multi is not installed because it is not necessary.

mysqld_multi looks for groups named [mysqldN] in my.cnf. Options listed in these groups are the same that you would use in the [mysqld] group used for starting mysqld. Nevertheless, when using multiple servers, it is necessary that each one use its own value for options such as the Unix socket file and TCP/IP port number.

To invoke mysqld_multi you should use the following syntax:

```
mysqld_multi [options
{start|stop|reload|report} [GNR[,GNR] …]
```

start, stop, reload, and report show which exact operation to perform. You can perform the designated operation for a single server or multiple servers, depending on the list that follows the option name. If there is no list, mysqld_multi completes the operation for all servers in the options file.

Each value represents an option group number or range of group numbers. The value should be the number at the end of the group name in the options file. Multiple groups or group ranges can be specified on the command line, separated by commas. There must be no whitespace characters (spaces or tabs) in the list as anything after a whitespace character is omitted.

This command starts a single server using option group [mysqld17]: mysqld_multi start 17

This command stops several servers, using option groups [mysqld8] and [mysqld10] through [mysqld13]: mysqld_multi stop 8,10-13

For an example of how you might set up an option file, use this command:

```
mysqld_multi -example
```

mysqld_multi searches for option files as follows:

- With -no-defaults, no option files are read.

- With -defaults-file=file_name, only the named file is read.

Otherwise, option files in the standard list of locations are read, including any file named by the --defaults-extra-file=file_name option. In case the option is given multiple times, the last value is used.

Option files read are searched for [mysqld_multi] and [mysqldN] option groups. The [mysqld_multi] group can be used for options to mysqld_multi itself. [mysqldN] groups can be used for options passed to specific mysqld instances.

The [mysqld] or [mysqld_safe] groups can be used for common options read by all instances of mysqld or mysqld_safe. You can specify a -defaults-file=file_name option to use a different configuration file for that instance, in which case the [mysqld] or [mysqld_safe] groups from that file are used for that instance.

Subsequently, mysqld_multi supports the following options:

- **help:** Used to display a help message and exit.

- **example:** Used to display a sample option file.

- **log=file_name:** Used to specify the name of the log file. If the file exists, log output is attached to it.

- **mysqladmin=prog_name:** Stands for the mysqladmin binary used to stop servers.

- **mysqld=prog_name:** Applied to specify the mysqld binary to be used. Additionally, you can specify mysqld_safe as the value for this option. If you use mysqld_safe to start the server, you can include the mysqld or ledir options in the connected [mysqldN] option group. These options indicate the name of the server that mysqld_safe should start and the path-name of the directory where the server is located. To illustrate with an example:

```
[mysqld38]
mysqld = mysqld-debug
ledir = /opt/local/mysql/libexec
```

- **no-log:** Used to print log information that by default goes to the log file.

- **password=password:** Stands for the password of the MySQL account to use when invoking mysqladmin. Note that the password value is obligatory for this option, unlike for other MySQL programs.

- **silent:** Used to activate the silent mode and disable warnings.

- **TCP-ip:** Applied to connect to each MySQL server through the TCP/IP port. By default, connections are made using the Unix socket file but not with this script. This option also affects stop and report operations.

- **user=user_name:** The user name of the MySQL account to use when activating mysqladmin.

- **verbose:** Used to seem more verbose.

- **version:** Used to display version information and exit.

Important to mention that before using mysqld_multi, you need to be sure that you understand the meanings of the options that are passed to the mysqld servers and why you would want to keep separate mysqld processes. One has to be aware of the dangers of using multiple mysqld servers with the same data directory and potentially use separate data directories, unless aware of the process. As well, starting multiple servers with the same data directory does not typically result in advanced performance in a threaded system.

In addition, make sure that the MySQL account used for stopping the mysqld servers has the same user name and password for each server as well as the SHUTDOWN privilege. If the servers that you want to manage have different user names or passwords for the administrative accounts, you might have to create an account on each server that has the same user name and password. For instance, you might set up a common multi_admin account by implementing the following commands for each server:[4]

```
shell> MySQL -u root -S/tmp/MySQL.sock -p
Enter password:
mysql> CREATE USER 'multi_admin'@'localhost'
IDENTIFIED BY 'multipass';
mysql> GRANT SHUTDOWN ON *.* TO
'multi_admin'@'localhost';
```

And just to be clear, you have to do this for each mysqld server. Change the connection parameters appropriately when connecting to each one. The hostname part of the account name must permit you to connect as multi_admin from the host where you want to run mysqld_multi.

The Unix socket file and the TCP/IP port number must be different for every mysqld. Alternatively, if the host has multiple network addresses, you can add the bind_address system variable to cause different servers to listen to different interfaces.

The --PID-file option is very important if you are using mysqld_safe to start mysqld. Every mysqld should have its own process ID file. The advantage of using mysqld_safe instead of

---

[4] https://dev.mysql.com/doc/refman/8.0/en/mysqld-multi.html, MySQL

mysqld is that mysqld_safe observes its mysqld process and restarts it if the process ends due to segmentation fault.

*mysql_upgrade—Check and Upgrade MySQL Tables*
Every time you upgrade MySQL, you should implement mysql_upgrade, which looks for incompatibilities with the upgraded MySQL server in addition to the following functions:

- It upgrades the system tables in the MySQL schema so that you can use new privileges or capabilities that might have been added.

- It upgrades the Performance Schema, INFORMATION_SCHEMA, and sys schema.

- It examines and tests user schemas.

- If mysql_upgrade finds that a table has a possible incompatibility, it activates a table check and, if problems are found, completes a table repair. mysql_upgrade is directly connected to the MySQL server, sending it the SQL statements required to start an upgrade.

Another thing one should keep in mind is to always secure your current MySQL installation before performing an upgrade. Some upgrade incompatibilities may take special handling before upgrading your MySQL installation and running mysql_upgrade.

Use mysql_upgrade to ensure that the server is running and only then invoke mysql_upgrade to upgrade the system tables in the MySQL schema and check and repair tables in other schemas with the mysql_upgrade [options] variable. Afterward, you can stop the server and restart it so that any system table changes take effect.

If you have multiple MySQL server items to upgrade, you can make use of mysql_upgrade with connection parameters suitable for connecting to each of the servers. For instance, with servers running on the localhost on parts 3401 through 3403, upgrade each of them by connecting to the appropriate port:[5]

```
mysql_upgrade --protocol=tcp -P 3401
[other_options]
mysql_upgrade --protocol=tcp -P 3402
[other_options]
mysql_upgrade --protocol=tcp -P 3403
[other_options]
For local host connections on Uni
x, the -protocol=tcp option forces a
connection using TCP/IP rather than the
Unix socket file.
```

By default, mysql_upgrade runs as the MySQL root user. Once the root password gets expired when you run mysql_upgrade, it shall send a message that your password is expired and that mysql_upgrade failed due to that. To fix this, reset the root password to unexpire it and run mysql_upgrade again. First, connect to the server as root:

```
shell> MySQL -u root -p
Enter password: **** <- enter root password
here
```

---

[5] https://dev.mysql.com/doc/refman/8.0/en/mysqld-multi.html, MySQL

```
Reset the password using ALTER USER:
mysql> ALTER USER USER() IDENTIFIED BY
'root-password';
```

Then exit MySQL and run mysql_upgrade again: shell> mysql_upgrade [options]

Keep in mind that If you run the server with the dis-abled_storage_engines system variable set to disable certain storage engines, mysql_upgrade might fail with an error like this:

```
mysql_upgrade: [ERROR] 3161: Storage engine
MyISAM is disabled.
```

To manage this, restart the server with disabled_stor-age_engines disabled. Then you should be able to activate mysql_upgrade successfully. Once done, restart the server with disabled_storage_engines set to its original value.

Unless invoked with the --upgrade-system-tables option, mysql_upgrade processes all tables in all user schemas as necessary. Table checking might take a long time to complete as each table is locked and therefore unavailable to other sessions while it is being processed. Therefore, check and repair procedures can be time-consuming, particularly for large tables. Table checking uses the FOR UPGRADE option of the CHECK TABLE statement.

mysql_upgrade defines all checked and repaired tables with the current MySQL version number. This ensures that the next time you run mysql_upgrade with the same version of the server, it can be seen whether there is any need to check or repair a given table again.

mysql_upgrade also saves the MySQL version number in a file named mysql_upgrade_info in the data directory. This is used to rapidly check whether all tables have been checked for this release so that table-checking can be omitted. To ignore this file and complete the check regardless, you can apply the -force option.

mysql_upgrade checks MySQL.user system table rows and, for any row that has an empty plugin column, transforms that column into 'mysql_native_password' if the credentials use a hash format consistent with that plugin. However, rows with a pre-4.1 password hash should be upgraded manually.

At the same time, mysql_upgrade does not upgrade the contents of the time zone tables or help tables. So unless invoked with the --skip-sys-schema option, mysql_upgrade installs the sys schema if it is not installed, and then upgrades it to the current version. An error occurs if a sys schema exists but has no version view, on the assumption that its absence indicates a user-created schema. In addition, sys schema can manage without sys.version view. If you have a user-created sys schema, it must be renamed for the upgrade to succeed. To upgrade in this case, remove or rename the existing sys schema first.

mysql_upgrade supports the following script options, that can be inserted on the command line or in the [mysql_upgrade] and [client] groups of an option file:[6]

---

[6] https://dev.mysql.com/doc/refman/8.0/en/mysql-command-options.html, MySQL

| Option Name | Description |
| --- | --- |
| bind-address | Use specified network interface to connect to MySQL Server |
| character-sets-dir | Directory where character sets are installed |
| compress | Compress all information sent between client and server |
| compression-algorithms | Permitted compression algorithms for connections to server |
| debug | Write debugging log |
| debug-check | Print debugging information when program exits |
| debug-info | Print debugging information, memory, and CPU statistics when program exits |
| default-auth | Authentication plugin to use |
| default-character-set | Specify default character set |
| defaults-extra-file | Read named option file in addition to usual option files |
| defaults-file | Read only named option file |
| defaults-group-suffix | Option group suffix value |
| force | Force execution even if mysql_upgrade has already been executed for current MySQL version |
| get-server-public-key | Request RSA public key from server |
| help | Display help message and exit |
| host | Host on which MySQL server is located |
| login-path | Read login path options from .mylogin.cnf |
| max-allowed-packet | Maximum packet length to send to or receive from server net |
| buffer-length | Buffer size for TCP/IP and socket communication |
| no-defaults | Read no option files |
| password | Password to use when connecting to server |
| pipe | Connect to server using named pipe (Windows only) |

*(Continued)*

| Option Name | Description |
| --- | --- |
| plugin-dir | Directory where plugins are installed |
| port | TCP/IP port number for connection |
| print-defaults | Print default options |
| protocol | Transport protocol to use |
| server-public-key-path | Path name to file containing RSA public key |
| shared-memory-base-name | Shared-memory name for shared-memory connections |
| skip-sys-schema | Do not install or upgrade sys schema |
| socket | Unix socket file or Windows named pipe to use |
| ssl-ca | File that contains list of trusted SSL Certificate Authorities |
| ssl-capath | Directory that contains trusted SSL Certificate Authority certificate files |
| ssl-cert | File that contains X.509 certificate |
| ssl-cipher | Permissible ciphers for connection encryption |
| ssl-crl | File that contains certificate revocation lists |
| ssl-crlpath | Directory that contains certificate revocation-list files |
| ssl-fips-mode | Whether to enable FIPS mode on client side |
| ssl-key | File that contains X.509 key |
| ssl-mode | Desired security state of connection to server |
| tls-ciphersuites | Permissible TLSv1.3 ciphersuites for encrypted connections |
| tls-version | Permissible TLS protocols for encrypted connections |
| upgrade-system-tables | Update only system tables, not user schemas |

*(Continued)*

| Option Name | Description |
| --- | --- |
| user | MySQL user name to use when connecting to server |
| verbose | Verbose mode |
| version-check | Check for proper server version |
| write-binlog | Write all statements to binary log |
| zstd-compression-level | Compression level for connections to server that use zstd compression |

- **help:** Used to display a short help message and exit.

- **bind-address=ip_address:** Mostly applied on a computer that has multiple network interfaces to select which interface to use for connecting to the MySQL server.

- **character-sets-dir=dir_name:** The directory where character sets are installed.

- **compress, -C:** Used to compress all information sent between the client and the server.

- **compression-algorithms=value:** Stands for the permitted compression algorithms for connections to the server. The available algorithms are similar to the protocol_compression_algorithms system variable. The default value is uncompressed.

- **debug[=debug_options], -# [debug_options]:** Used to write a debugging log. A typical debug_options string is d:t:o,file_name. The default is d:t:O,/tmp/mysql_upgrade.trace.

- **debug-check:** Applied when printing some debugging information needed.

- **debug-info, -T:** Used to print debugging information and memory usage statistics when the program exits.

- **default-auth=plugin:** Displays a hint about which client-side authentication plugin to use.

- **default-character-set=charset_name:** Applied when you would need to use charset_name as the default character set.

- **defaults-extra-file=file_name:** Read this option file after the global option file but before the user option file. If the file is inaccessible, an error occurs; and if file_name is not an absolute pathname, it is interpreted relative to the current directory.

- **defaults-file=file_name:** Similar to the previous directory, if the file does not exist or is otherwise inaccessible, the server exits with an error. If file_name is not an absolute pathname, it is interpreted relative to the current directory.

- **defaults-group-suffix=str:** Applied when it is necessary to read not only the usual option groups but also groups with the usual names and a suffix of str. For instance, mysql_upgrade normally reads the [client] and [mysql_upgrade] groups. If this option is given as --defaults-group-suffix=_other, mysql_upgrade also reads the [client_other] and [mysql_upgrade_other] groups.

- **force:** Ignores the mysql_upgrade_info file and forces execution even if mysql_upgrade has already been implemented for the current version of MySQL.

- **get-server-public-key:** Used to request the server for the public key required for key pair-based password exchange. This option applies to clients that authenticate with the caching_sha2_password authentication plugin. For that plugin, the server does not provide the public key unless requested. Nevertheless, this option is ignored for accounts that do not authenticate with that plugin. It is also deactivated if key pair-based password exchange is not used, for example, when the client links to the server using a secure connection only.

  Note that in case --server-public-key-path=file_ name is defined as a valid public key file it would have to take precedence over --get-server-public-key.

- **host=host_name, -h host_name:** Connects to the MySQL server on any given host.

- **login-path=name:** Used to read options from the named login path in the. mylogin.cnf login path file. A "login path" here stands for an option group holding options that dictate which MySQL server to connect to and which account to verify. To create or edit a login path file, use the mysql_config_editor instead.

- **max-allowed-packet=value:** Stands for the maximum size of the buffer for client/server communication. The default value is normally 24 MB. The minimum and maximum values are 4 KB and 2 GB.

- **net-buffer-length=value:** Stands for the initial size of the buffer for client/server communication. The default value is average between 1 MB to 1 KB. The minimum and maximum values are 4 KB and 16 MB.

- **no-defaults:** Do not read any option files. If program startup fails due to reading unknown options from an option file, --no-defaults can be applied to prevent them from being read. The exception is that the .mylogin.cnf file is read in all cases if it exists. This permits passwords to be specified in a safer way than on the command line even when --no-defaults is used. To create .mylogin.cnf, use the mysql_config_editor utility.

- **password[=password], -p[password]:** Stands for the password of the MySQL account used for connecting to the server. The password value is optional, but if not given, mysql_upgrade comes up with one anyway. If given, there must be no space between --password= or -p and the password following it.

  Consider specifying a password on the command line insecure. To avoid giving the password on the command line, use an option file. To explicitly state that there is no password and that mysql_upgrade should not prompt for one, use the --skip-password option.

- **pipe, -W:** Used to establish a connection to the server using a named pipe on Windows. This option applies only if the server was activated with the named_pipe system variable enabled to support named-pipe connections. Moreover, the user creating the connection should be a member of the Windows group specified by the named_pipe_full_access_group system variable.

- **plugin-dir=dir_name:** The directory applied to search for plugins. You can make use of this option if the --default-auth option was specified by an authentication plugin but mysql_upgrade did not find it.

- **port=port_num, -P port_num:** For TCP/IP connections, the port number to use.

- **print-defaults:** Applied to print the program name and all options that it gets from option files.

- **protocol={TCP|SOCKET|PIPE|MEMORY}:** The transport protocol to use for connecting to the server. It is particularly practical when the other connection parameters resulted in the use of a protocol other than the one you wanted.

- **server-public-key-path=file_name:** The pathname to a file in Privacy Enhanced Mail format containing a client-side copy of the public key required by the server for RSA key pair-based password exchange. This option applies to users that authenticate with the sha256_password or caching_sha2_password authentication plugin. But it is typically ignored for accounts that do not authenticate with one of those plugins. It is also ignored if key pair-based password exchange is not applied, as is the case when the user connects to the server directly through a secure connection.

- **shared-memory-base-name=name:** Used for the shared-memory name to make connections made through shared memory of a local server. The default value is MYSQL with the shared-memory name being case-sensitive. However, this option applies only on Windows with a server started through the shared_memory system variable.

- **skip-sys-schema:** By default, mysql_upgrade installs the sys schema if it is not installed, and upgrades it to the current version otherwise. This --skip-sys-schema option suppresses this pattern.

- **socket=path, -S path:** Used to connect to localhost, or to determine which named pipe to use. On Windows, this option applies only if the server was activated with the named_pipe system variable enabled to support named-pipe connections. Moreover, the user establishing the connection should be a member of the Windows group defined by the named_pipe_full_access_group system variable.

- **SSL:** Scripts that begin with --SSL specifies whether to connect to the server using encryption and show where to find SSL keys and certificates.

- **ssl-fips-mode={OFF|ON|STRICT}:** States whether to enable Federal Information Processing Standards (FIPS) mode on the client-side or not. The --ssl-fips-mode option is not the same as other --SSL-xxx options in that it is not used to create encrypted connections, but rather to affect which operations to proceed with.

These --SSL-fips-mode values are permitted:

- **OFF:** Disable Federal Information Processing Standards mode.

- **ON:** Enable Federal Information Processing Standards mode.

- **STRICT:** Enable "strict" Federal Information Processing Standards mode.

If you see the OpenSSL FIPS Object Module is not available, the only permitted value for --SSL-fips-mode is OFF. In this case, setting --ssl-fips-mode to ON or STRICT causes the client to come up with a warning at startup and to work in non-FIPS mode.

- **tls-ciphersuites=ciphersuite_list:** The script provides the list of permissible ciphersuites for encrypted connections that use Transport Layer Security 1.3. The value results in one or more colon-separated ciphersuite names. The ciphersuites that can be named for this option depend on the SSL library used to compile MySQL.

- **tls-version=protocol_list:** Provide variants of permissible Transport Layer Security protocols for encrypted connections. The value is a list of one or more comma-separated protocol names. The protocols that can be named for this option depend on the SSL library used to set MySQL.

- **upgrade-system-tables, -s:** Used to upgrade only the system tables in the MySQL schema and not the user schemas.

- **user=user_name, -u user_name:** Stand for the user name of the MySQL account to apply for connecting to the server. The default user name is root.

- **verbose:** Used to activate the verbose mode.

- **version-check, -k:** Great to complete a checkup of the server version to which mysql_upgrade is connecting to verify that it is the same as the version for which mysql_upgrade was built. If not, mysql_upgrade exits by default. If you want to disable the check, use --skip-version-check.

- **write-binlog:** Since binary logging by mysql_upgrade is disabled by default, you should activate the program with --write-binlog if you need its actions to be written to the binary log. However, if you see the server running with global transaction identifiers (GTIDs) enabled (gtid_mode=ON), do not enable binary logging by mysql_upgrade.

- **zstd-compression-level=level:** Stands for the compression level to use for connections to the server that employ the zstd compression algorithm. The permitted levels are from 1 to 22, with larger values defining increasing levels of compression. The default zstd compression level is 3. At the same time, the compression level setting has no impact on connections that do not apply zstd compression whatsoever.

## RUNNING A SQL FILE

MySQL is a quite simple SQL shell with extensive input line editing capacities. It supports both interactive and noninteractive use. if used interactively, query results are displayed in an ASCII-table format. And when used noninteractively, the result is presented in tab-separated format.

In case you face problems due to inefficient memory for large result combinations you can apply the --quick option. This makes MySQL to retrieve output from the server a row at a time rather than retrieving the entire result combinations and buffering it in memory before delivering it. This is completed by returning the result combination using the mysql_use_result function in the client/server library rather than mysql_store_result.

Using MySQL is very pretty straightforward as it is. Call it from the prompt of your command interpreter as follows:

```
MySQL db_name
Or:
MySQL --user=user_name --password db_name
```

In the second case, you will have to enter your password in response to the prompt that MySQL displays:

Enter password: your_password

Then type an SQL statement, end it with;, \g, or \G and press Enter. Typing Control+C disturbs the current statement if there is one, or breaks in any partial input line otherwise.

In addition, it is also possible to execute SQL statements in a script file similar to:

```
MySQL db_name < script.sql > output.tab
```

The MySQL client typically is used interactively in the following format: MySQL db_name. But you can also insert your SQL statements in a file and then dictate MySQL read its input from that file. To do so, create a text file text_file that holds the statements you wish to implement. Then activate MySQL with MySQL db_name < text_file. And if you put a USE db_name statement as the first statement in the file, it would then be unnecessary to specify the database name on the command line: MySQL < text_file.

If you are already running MySQL, you can implement an SQL script file with the following source command:

```
mysql> source file_name
mysql> \. file_name
```

Sometimes you might need your script to show progress information to the user. For this you can add statements like this:

```
SELECT '<info_to_display>' AS ' ';
```

The statement shown outputs <info_to_display>.

You can also include MySQL with the --verbose option, which causes each statement to be displayed before the result that it comes up with.

Worth noting that MySQL ignores Unicode byte order mark characters at the beginning of input files. Previously, it read them and forward them to the server, resulting in a syntax error. Inclusion of a byte order mark characters does not make MySQL to change its default character combination. To do that, invoke MySQL with a script option such as --default-character-set=utf8.

## EDITING DATA

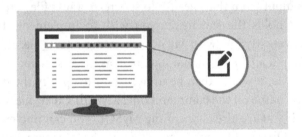

The MySQL Table Editor is used to generate and edit tables. You can add or modify the columns or indexes of a table, change the engine, add foreign keys, or revise the table name. I order to access the MySQL Table Editor, right-click a table name in the Navigator area of the sidebar with the Schemas secondary tab selected and click Alter Table. This action opens a new secondary tab within the main SQL Editor window. You can also activate the MySQL Table Editor from an Enhanced entity-relationship (EER) Diagram by double-clicking on a table object.

Any number of tables may be edited in the MySQL Table Editor at any given time. Adding another table results in a new secondary tab at the top of the editor. By default, the MySQL Table Editor is placed at the top of the table editor tab, within the SQL editor. It typically provides a workspace that has subtabs used to complete the following actions:[7]

- **Columns:** Add or adjust columns

- **Indexes:** Add or alter indexes

- **Foreign Keys:** Add or modify foreign keys

- **Triggers:** Add or edit triggers

- **Partitioning:** Manage partitioning of a table

- **Options:** Add or change other options, divided into categories named general, row, storage, and merge

Columns Tab

You can use the Columns subtab to present and edit all the column data for a table. With this subtab, you can add, cancel, or change columns. You can also apply the Columns subtab to alter column properties such as name, data type, and default value. Just right-click a row under the Column Name to review a pop-up menu with the following list:[8]

- **Move Up:** Move the selected column up.

- **Move Down:** Move the selected column down.

---

[7] https://dev.mysql.com/doc/workbench/en/wb-table-editor-main-window.html, MySQL

[8] https://dev.mysql.com/doc/workbench/en/wb-table-editor-main-window.html, MySQL

- **Copy:** Copies the column for a model.

- **Cut:** Copies and then deletes the column for a model.

- **Paste:** Pastes the column. If a column with the same name already exists, then _copy1 is appended to the column name.

- **Delete Selected Columns:** Select multiple contiguous columns by right-clicking and pressing the Shift key. Use the Control key to select separated columns.

- **Refresh:** Update all information in the Columns subtab.

- **Clear Default:** Clear the assigned default value.

- **Default NULL:** Set the column default value to NULL.

- **Default 0:** Set the column default value to 0.

- **Default CURRENT_TIMESTAMP:** Available for TIMESTAMP data types.

- **Default CURRENT_TIMESTAMP ON UPDATE CURRENT_TIMESTAMP:** Available for TIMESTAMP data types.

If you need to add a column, click the Column Name option in an empty row and enter an appropriate value. Then choose a data type from the Datatype list and the column property checkboxes as required according to the list of column properties that follow:[9]

---

[9] https://dev.mysql.com/doc/workbench/en/wb-table-editor-main-window. html, MySQL

- **PK:** PRIMARY KEY

- **NN:** NOT NULL

- **UQ:** UNIQUE INDEX

- **BIN:** BINARY

- **UN:** UNSIGNED

- **ZF:** ZEROFILL

- **AI:** AUTO_INCREMENT

- **G:** Generated Column

In order to change properties like the name, data type, default value, or comment of a column, you just have to double-click at its value and edit it. You can also add column comments to the Column Comment field. In addition, you can also set the column collation, using the list in the Column Details panel.

To the left of the column name, you should be able to see an icon that shows whether the column is a member of the primary key. If the icon is a small key, that column belongs to the primary key, otherwise, the icon is a blue diamond or a white diamond. A blue diamond defines that the column has NN set. To add or delete a column from the primary key, just double-click the icon. It is also possible to add a primary key by checking the PRIMARY KEY check box in the Column Details section of the table editor.

If you need to create a composite primary key, you should go ahead and select multiple columns and click the PK check box. However, there is an additional step in which you should click the Indexes tab, then in the Index Columns panel, you have to set the proper order of the primary keys.

## Indexes Tab

The Indexes subtab holds all of the index data for your table. You can use this subtab to add, drop, and edit indexes. All indexes for a table are displayed by index name. Simply click an index name to see all the Index Columns section with information about the selected index. In addition, in the same section, you should be able to modify the storage type, key block size, parser, and visibility of the index. Index comments, when included, apply to the selected index only. To add an index, click the last row in the index list and insert a name for the index as well as the index type from the list. You should also choose the column or multiple columns that you need to index by checking the column name in the Index Columns list. You can delete a column from the index just by removing the checkmark from the applicable column.

In order to specify the order of a column within an index, pick ASC or DESC from the Order column. Next, create an index prefix by defining a numeric value under the Length column. You will not be able to enter a prefix value for fields that have a data type that does not support prefixing.

If you want to render a secondary index that is invisible to the optimizer, just deselect the Visible option. By default, all indexes are made visible, so this feature has to be supported by the active server; otherwise, the Visible check box will be omitted. In addition, to drop an index, simply right-click the index name and then click the Delete Selected menu option.

## Foreign Keys Tab

The Foreign Keys subtab is structure is pretty much the same way as the Indexes subtab, meaning that adding or editing a foreign key is similar to adding or editing an index.

To add a foreign key, click the last row in the Foreign Key Name list. Here, enter a name for the foreign key and select the column or multiple columns that you want to index by checking the column name in the Column list. You can delete a column from the index simply by removing the checkmark from the column. Under Foreign Key Options, you can choose an action for the update and delete events. The options are[10]

- RESTRICT

- CASCADE

- SET NULL

- NO ACTION

If you wish to drop a foreign key, right-click the row you wish to remove and then click on the Delete Selected FKs

---

[10] https://dev.mysql.com/doc/workbench/en/wb-table-editor-foreign-keys-tab.html, MySQL

menu item. To edit the properties of a foreign key, you should just select it and make the desired changes.

## Triggers Tab

The Triggers subtab creates a work platform that enables you to generate new triggers or edit existing triggers. All triggers are placed within a tree structure by section, such as BEFORE INSERT and AFTER INSERT.

To add a new trigger, click the [+] icon next to the trigger section. To delete a trigger, simply click the assigned [-] icon. These icons become visible by layering over a trigger or trigger section. When finished click Apply to set your changes.

## Partitioning Tab

To activate partitioning for your table, check the Enable Partitioning check box. The Partition By pop-up menu presents the types of partitions you can choose from:[11]

- HASH

- LINEAR HASH

- KEY

- LINEAR KEY

- RANGE

- LIST

---

[11] https://dev.mysql.com/doc/workbench/en/wb-table-editor-partitioning-tab.html, MySQL

You can use the Parameters section to review all the parameters to be supplied to the partitioning function, similar to an integer column value. You can also choose the number of partitions from the Partition Count list. To manually modify your partitions, check the Manual check box to enter values into the partition configuration table. The available entries in this table are[12]

- Partition

- Values

- Data Directory

- Index Directory

- Min Rows

- Max Rows

- Comment

- Options Tab

Next, follow the Options subtab to set several types of options. Table options are categorized into the following sections:[13]

- General Options

- Row Options

---

[12] https://dev.mysql.com/doc/workbench/en/wb-table-editor-partitioning-tab.html, MySQL

[13] https://dev.mysql.com/doc/workbench/en/wb-table-editor-partitioning-tab.html, MySQL

- Storage Options

- Merge Table Options

In the General Options section, start by selecting a pack keys option. The options are Default, Pack None, and Pack All. You can also encrypt the definition of a table. However, the AUTO_INCREMENT and delayed key update patterns apply only to MyISAM tables.

Choose the Row Options Section to set the desired row format from the list. These options are: Default Dynamic Fixed Compressed Redundant Compact. When you need your table to be particularly large or small, make use of the Avg. Row, Min. Rows, and Max functions.

The Storage Options section is available only for MyISAM tables. You can use it to modify a custom path to the table storage and data files. This can ensure better server performance by transferring different tables to different hard drives.

You typically apply the Merge Table Options to configure MERGE tables. To establish a MERGE table, choose MERGE to be your main storage engine and then specify the MyISAM tables you need to merge in the Union Tables dialog. You may indicate the action the server should take when users try to perform INSERT statements on the merge table.

With this basic editing discourse, it is now safe to dive into specific MySQL creating and operating various users/ roles section, as well as touch upon the part that explains how to import and export the database.

# Server Administration

DOI: 10.1201/9781003229629-5

A server is a computer or system that supplies and delivers resources, data, services, or programs to other computers, also known as clients, over a network. In theory, whenever computers distribute resources to client machines, they are considered servers. However, as technology has evolved, such a definition of a server has evolved with it. Currently, a server might be nothing more than software running on one or more physical computing devices. Servers as such are often referred to as virtual servers. Originally, virtual servers were used to increase the number of server functions a single hardware server could complete. Today, virtual servers are often operated by a third party on hardware across the Internet in a formation named cloud computing.

A server could be designed to complete a single task, such as a mail server, which accepts and stores email and then provides it to a requesting client. Or it can also perform several tasks, such as a file and print server, which both can store files and accept print jobs from clients and then forward them on to a network-attached printer.

Typically, to operate as a server, a device should be configured to listen to requests from clients on a network connection. This characteristic can exist as part of the operating system as an installed application, role, or a combination of the two. For instance, Microsoft's Windows Server operating system provides the functionality to listen to and respond to client requests. In addition, installed roles or services expand the types of client requests the server can respond to. To illustrate with an example, an Apache web server responds to Internet browser requests via an additional application, Apache, installed on top of an operating system.

When a client needs data or functionality from a server, it forwards a request over the network. The server receives this request and responds with the appropriate information. This is the request and response model of client-server networking, also known as the call and response model. Additionally, a server will often perform numerous extra tasks as part of a single request and response, including certifying the identity of the requestor, making sure that the client has permission to access the data or resources requested, and properly modifying or returning the required response in an expected way. There are many types of servers that all complete different functions. Many networks hold one or more of the common server types:

- **File servers:** used to store and distribute files. Multiple clients or users may share files stored on a server. Moreover, centrally storing files has better backup or fault tolerance solutions than attempting to provide security and integrity for files on every device in an organization.

- **Print servers:** ensure effective management and distribution of printing functionality. Rather than attaching a printer to every workstation, it offers a single print server service to numerous requests from numerous clients. Normally, larger and higher-end printers come with their own built-in print server, which removes the need for an additional computer-based print server.

- **Application servers:** run applications in lieu of client computers administering applications locally.

Application servers often execute resource-intensive applications that are shared by a large number of users. Doing so eliminates the necessity for each client to have sufficient resources to run the applications. It also removes the need to install and maintain software on many devices as opposed to only one.

- **Domain Name System (DNS) servers:** provide name resolution to client computers by converting names that are user-friendly into machine-readable IP addresses. The DNS system is a widely distributed database of names and other DNS servers, each of which can be used to request an unknown computer name. When a client needs the address of a system, it sends a DNS request with the name of the desired resource to a DNS server. The DNS server responds with the necessary IP address from its table of names.

- **Mail servers:** used to receive emails sent to a user and store them until requested by a client. Having an email server lets a single machine be properly configured and attached to the network at all times. It is then ready to send and receive messages rather than requiring every client machine to have its own email subsystem constantly running.

- **Web servers:** is a special kind of application server that hosts programs and data requested by users across the Internet. Web servers usually respond to requests from browsers running on client computers for web pages, or other web-based services. Common web servers include Apache web servers, Microsoft Internet Information Services (IIS) servers, and Nginx servers.

- **Database servers:** run database applications and respond to numerous requests from clients. Mostly used by companies, databases need to be accessible to multiple clients at any given time and can require extraordinary amounts of disk space. This particular type of server would be the main topic of the next section.

Every day, we create an enormous amount of data bytes, and this number is only going to accelerate at an exponential rate in the near future. To illustrate, it is believed that we have collected more data for the past two years than in entire human history. And one of the basic locations where all this data is forwarded is a database. Without the database and capacity to query the database, it would be nearly impossible to collect and review any of that data in a comprehensive way. It is a truly groundbreaking time in the data world with a new system for data collection, manipulation, and types of databases. With this, you have different groups of gatekeepers and maintainers for all the datasets of information. You typically call these professionals database administrators (DBA) and server administrators.

DBA includes all the activities required to manage a database and maintain it available at all times. The DBA is the expert who operates, backs up, and guarantees the availability of the data produced and consumed by a given organization through their IT systems. The DBA is a crucial role in today's IT-driven enterprises and by extension, the modern world overall.

To illustrate, consider a standard commercial bank: the DBA is the profession that would have to make sure that the bank worker has fast access to any customer's information, and can quickly navigate the whole transaction history. In this example, the DBA stands for a system of the application-DBA responsible for most aspects of the organization's databases. However, this role has to be backed up and advanced in cooperation with proactive server management as well.

Server administrators typically take the case of the company's servers, network, and workstations, and are in charge of keeping the company's systems running constantly and error-free. For that, they have to install programs, update the operating system according to the latest trends and supervise the users' activities.

Server administrators also have to be the ones to keep an eye on data floating in and out of the network and be in charge of keeping the network secure, therefore they might at times respond to security concerns by tightening the firewall settings. In addition, the server administrator's responsibilities may also include the following:

- Installing and upgrading the database server and/or application products.

- Scheduling for and allocating the database system's physical requirements, such as memory, disk space, and network requirements.

- Adjusting the database structure using the information provided by application developers.

- Filing users' profiles and ensuring system security.

- Assuring compliance with database vendor license agreement, including a number of installations and licensing renewals.

- Creating a backup and recovery plan for the database, and regularly testing the backups to maintain usability.

- Monitoring technical support for both database systems and related products.

- Establishing reports by querying from the database. These reports can be in the form of pre-formatted statements using the application frontend, or custom-made ad hoc reports by the DBA.

- Auditing and optimizing the database's performance using both manual or automated tools.

- Migrating database instances to new hardware and new versions of software from on-premise to cloud-based databases and vice versa.

Moreover, there is a wide range of sub-specializations for the server administrator role. There are those who specialize in creating and designing databases in the first place. They typically work as part of a team, often in a more specialized software development company. And that database is likely to be a fragment of a larger application for some specific need. Server specialists as such more likely to work in collaboration with analysts and others who are intimately familiar with various operations to design the most suited application's functions and modules.

Another type of server administrator is the Performance Administrator that specializes in optimizing and upgrading the performance of various server databases. Database's internal structure holds information stored within tables that then can be optimized by use of indexes, which look like a book's table of contents. Professional's goal here is to ensure that the database is optimized to take advantage of the physical or virtual hardware on which it is located. This means it is necessary to be able to divide data across different disks, set up the database to sustainable use of memory, and optimize the network traffic of remote databases. There are also some databases that are split among multiple servers, while others can get so complex that they need a DBA who focuses only on that particular segment's performance improvement.

The third type of server administrator is the Application expert that focuses mainly on integrating databases into the applications that apply them. Navigating most databases usually requires knowledge of a specific type of query language. It is the responsibility of the application expert to make sure that the database and the application using it interconnect properly, and that accurate results are transmitted between the two.

Databases that we have mentioned so far are primarily one of three different types: flat-file databases, hierarchical databases, and relational databases. Flat-file databases have a minimalist, two-dimensional structure. Excel spreadsheets and comma-separated value files are a great depiction of flat-file databases. Hierarchical databases, on the other hand, have a parent-child relationship built into their structure. An example of a hierarchical database is a folder structure on a hard drive. Relational databases are the closest to what we now think of when we say database. It's like taking several of those flat-file databases and associating them together through references that they both share in common.

And since SQL Server is relational database software, it is necessary to start by exploring some of the basic relational database concepts.

A relational database includes one or more tables, with each table made up of one or more domains, and columns that briefly define the data being recorded. Each entry in the table is referred is an entity.

- **Normalization and information consolidation:** As previously stated, normalization is the result of the process of getting rid of redundancies in the data. It is an important concept and could be better described with the following example.

  Imagine you have a table that holds information about people, a simple thing to imagine is using a domain for the city. Let's assume that you have 10 people on your list, with five living in London and five living in Manchester.

  In order to normalize that data, you should create an additional table called cityname. Inside that table, "London" would be the first city with an ID of "1," and "Manchester" would be entered with an ID of "2." You would then update your people table to reference the city table instead of having the cities entered for each field. Even our simple example of ten people would benefit by having "London" at six characters and "Manchester" at ten characters replaced with an ID number that is only one character long.

- **Indexes preload:** An index can be arranged to provide faster access to certain key columns of data in a table, such as a title or a name field so that queries can be operated more quickly. And while each index that you define has an inherent cost associated with it, it is still worth identifying those fields that will be searched and structured so that they can be indexed.

- **Pages are the building blocks of SQL Server data storage:** The databases are located in files on disk. The same files are made up of 8 KB bits of data called pages. Every single row of data from a table has to fit inside a page. So that afterward pages could be loaded into memory to make a change to an entity.

- **Transaction logs:** Transaction logs are used to identify which changes have been made to a page since it was last saved to disk and hold a record of all the history, including even the smallest editions. This is to protect the data while it is in volatile Random-access memory instead of on the hard drive. In case of a power failure, SQL Server begins reviewing all of the unsaved changes back into memory.

- **Database data types:** Data can be stored in several different types. For instance, date/time, Numbers, True/False (Boolean), and Images are examples of different data types. Each data type originally has its own impact on the size of the database. Large numbers generally take more space than a simple true/false when stored on disk, so using the smallest data type possible might play well in the longer run.

- **Binary Large Objects (BLOBs):** BLOBs stands for items such as images, sound files, and attachments that are located on disk as separate files, where a pointer to the file is stored inside the table.

Another thing to refresh is the fact that the SQL language itself is broken into three different parts: Data Manipulation Language (DML), Data Definition Language (DDL), and Control Language.

- **DML:** DML is reserved for queries and updates of data in the tables. SELECT, INSERT, UPDATE, and DELETE are all commands from DML.

- **DDL:** DDL ensures control over the database itself instead of the rows of data in the database. USE, CREATE, and DROP are examples of DDL.

- **Control Language:** Control language includes logical structures for controlling flow, repetition, and if/then logic.

After going through existing SQL Server infrastructure and refreshing some basic knowledge of database administration, you are now ready for a thorough MySQL Server overview: fundamentals of multiple instances, training, and initial work with databases, data importing, and exporting.

## INSTANCES

The MySQL server, mysqld, has many command options and system variables that can should be applied at startup to modify its operation. To define the default command option and system variable values used by the server, insert the following command:

```
shell> mysqld --verbose --help
```

This command puts together a list of all mysqld options and configurable system variables. Its output includes the default option and variable values. And in case you want to see the current system variable values actually applied by the server as it runs, link to it and execute this statement:

```
mysql> SHOW VARIABLES;
```

In order to review some statistical and status indicators for a running server, implement this statement:

```
mysql> SHOW STATUS;
```

In addition, various system variables and status information are also available using the mysqladmin command:

```
shell> mysqladmin variables
shell> mysqladmin extended-status
```

An instance could be defined as any server program accessing MySQL program on the server-side at a given time. It is possible to use a different MySQL server binary per instance, or use the same binary for multiple instances, or any set of the two approaches. An instance of the Database Engine is a duplication of the sqlservr.exe executable that administers as an operating system service. Each instance runs several system databases and one or more user databases. As well as that, each computer can run multiple instances of the Database Engine independently of other instances.

It is easy to install and edit multiple instances of SQL Server on the same machine. You can make multiple named instances and store the system database, and log files in separate directories. Once SQL Server instances are set, you can connect them by identifying the HOSTNAME/INSTANCE name in the connection string of the application server or the SQL Server Management Studio (SSMS).

In some cases, you might need to run multiple instances of MySQL on a single machine, or you might need to test a new MySQL release while keeping an existing production setup undisturbed. Or it could also be true that you might want to give different users access to different mysqld servers that they run themselves (e.g., you could act as an Internet Service Provider that wants to provide independent MySQL installations for users).

It is, nevertheless, manageable to use a different MySQL server binary per instance or apply the same binary for multiple instances, or any combination of the two. For example, you might administer a server from MySQL 5.7 and one from MySQL 8.0, to see how different versions manage a certain workload. Or you might run multiple instances of the current production version, each managing a different set of databases.

Depending on whether or not you use distinct server binaries, each instance that you conduct must be configured with unique values for several operating standards. This would prevent any potential occurrence of conflict between instances. Parameters can be issued on the command line, in option files, or by setting environment variables.

The main resource managed by a MySQL instance is the data directory. Each instance should use a different data directory, the location of which is identified using the --datadir=dir_name option. In addition to using different data directories, several other options should also have different values for each server instance:[1]

- **port=port_num:** port regulates the port number for TCP/IP connections. At the same time, if the host has multiple network addresses, you can add the bind_address system variable to let each server listen to a different address.

- **socket={file_name|pipe_name}:** socket manages the Unix socket file path on Unix or the named-pipe name on Windows. On Windows, it is mandatory to define distinct pipe names only for those servers made to permit named-pipe links.

- **shared-memory-base-name=name:** This option is available only for Windows. It determines the shared-memory name used by a Windows server to allow clients to connect using shared memory. It is mandatory to specify distinct shared-memory names only for those servers configured to enable shared-memory connections.

- **pid-file=file_name:** This option suggests the pathname of the file in which the server writes its process ID.

---

[1] https://dev.mysql.com/doc/refman/8.0/en/multiple-servers.html, MySQL

If you use the following log file options, their values must differ for each server:

```
--general_log_file=file_name
--log-bin[=file_name]
--slow_query_log_file=file_name
--log-error[=file_name]
```

Additionally, to get better execution, you can specify the following option differently for each server, to share the load between several physical disks:

```
--tmpdir=dir_name
```

Having different temporary directories also makes it simpler to decide which MySQL server created any given temporary file. Thus, if you have multiple MySQL installations in different locations, you can select the base directory for each installation with the --basedir=dir_name option. This shall impact each instance and install automatic use of a different data directory, log files, and PID file because the default for each of those items would be relative to the base directory. In that case, the only other options you need to designate explicitly are the --socket and --port options. Imagine that you need to install different versions of MySQL using tar file binary distributions. These install in different locations, so you can start the server for each installation using the command bin/mysqld_safe under its corresponding base directory. mysqld_safe will select the proper --basedir option to pass to myself, and you would have to specify only the --socket and --port options to mysqld_safe.

As mentioned previously, it is possible to start additional servers by specifying best-suited command options or by setting environment variables. Nevertheless, if you need to operate multiple servers on a more persistent basis, it is more convenient to apply option files to specify for each server those option values that should be unique to it. The --defaults-file option is useful for this purpose.

It is by default that each MySQL Instance on a machine should have its own data directory. The location is typically identified using the --datadir=dir_name option. Correspondingly, there are different methods of setting up a data directory for a new instance: by creating a new data directory or by copying an already existing data directory.

## Creating a New Data Directory

With this approach, the data directory would be in the same state as when you first installed MySQL and would stay according to the default set of MySQL accounts and no user data.

To activate it on Unix, you just need to initialize the data directory. On Windows, the data directory is already included in the MySQL distribution. Thus, MySQL Zip archive distributions for Windows hold an unmodified data directory. You can unpack such distribution into a temporary location, then copy it data directory to where you are planning the new instance to be.

Windows MSI package installers create the data directory that the installed server uses, but also make a pristine "template" data directory named data under the installation directory. After an installation has been completed using an MSI package, the template data directory can be used to set up additional MySQL instances.

## Copying an Existing Data Directory

According to this approach, any MySQL accounts or user data present in the data directory can be simply carried over to the new data directory.

However, to start with, you need to stop the existing MySQL instance using the data directory. Then, copy the data directory to the location where the new data directory should be. And copy the my.cnf or my.ini option file used by the existing instance that later would serve as a basis for the new instance.

It is also important to modify the new option file so that any pathnames addressing the original data directory refer to the new data directory. Also, modify any other options that must be unique per instance, such as the TCP/IP port number and the log files. Only after that, you can start the new instance, telling it to use the new option file.

It is also possible to run multiple servers on Windows by starting them manually from the command line, each with appropriate operating standards, or via the installation of several servers as Windows services. We shall look through these options in detail in the following section.

## Starting Multiple MySQL Instances at the Windows Command Line

To start multiple servers using this method, you should specify the appropriate options on the command line or in an option file. It is more suitable to place the options in an option file, but it is also critical to make sure that each server has its own set of options. To achieve this, create an option file for each server and tell the server the file name with a --defaults-file option when you operate it.

Suppose that you want to run one instance of mysqld on port 4405 with a data directory of C:\mydata1, and another instance on port 4406 with a data directory of C:\mydata2. Use this procedure:[2]

Make sure that each data directory exists, including its own copy of the MySQL database that contains the grant tables. Then go into creating two option files. For instance, one file named C:\my-opts1.cnf that looks like this:

```
[mysqld]
datadir = C:/mydata1
port = 4405
```

And a second file named C:\my-opts2.cnf that looks like this:

```
[mysqld]
datadir = C:/mydata2
port = 4406
```

You can also use the --defaults-file option to start each server with its own option file:[3]

```
C:\> C:\mysql\bin\mysqld --defaults-
file=C:\my-opts1.cnf
C:\> C:\mysql\bin\mysqld --defaults-
file=C:\my-opts2.cnf
```

---

[2] https://dev.mysql.com/doc/refman/8.0/en/multiple-windows-command-line-servers.html, MySQL

[3] https://dev.mysql.com/doc/refman/8.0/en/multiple-windows-command-line-servers.html, MySQL

Each server would start in the foreground, so there would be no need to issue those two commands in separate console windows.

To stop the servers, you just need to connect to each using the appropriate port number:

```
C:\> C:\mysql\bin\mysqladmin --port=3307
--host=127.0.0.1 --user=root --password
shutdown
C:\> C:\mysql\bin\mysqladmin --port=3308
--host=127.0.0.1 --user=root --password
shutdown
```

In case your version of Windows supports named pipes and you also want to allow named-pipe connections, specify options that enable the named pipe and specify its name. Each server that supports named-pipe connections should be using a unique pipe name. TO illustrate, the C:\ my-opts1.cnf file could be written like this:

```
[mysqld]
datadir = C:/mydata1
port = 3307
enable-named-pipe
socket = mypipe1
```

You can modify C:\my-opts2.cnf in a similar manner to use by the second server.

A similar procedure applies for servers that you want to permit shared-memory connections. You can activate such connections by starting the server with the shared_memory system variable enabled and designate a unique shared-memory name for each server by setting the shared_memory_base_name system variable.

## Starting Multiple MySQL Instances as Windows Services

On Windows, a MySQL server can also operate as a Windows service. To set up multiple MySQL services, you need to make sure that each instance applies a different service name in addition to the other parameters that have to be kept unique per instance.

Imagine you need to run the mysqld server from two different versions of MySQL that are installed at C:\mysql-5.7.9 and C:\mysql-8.0.25, respectively. To install MySQL as a Windows service, use the --install or --install-manual option. Based on the above-mentioned information, you have several ways to set up multiple services. But before trying any of them, you need to shut down and remove any existing MySQL services.

- **Method 1:** Start by specifying the options for all services in one of the standard option files. To complete this, apply a different service name for each server. Suppose that you want to run the 5.7.9 mysqld using the service name of mysqld1 and the 8.0.25 mysqld using the service name mysqld2. In this case, you can use the [mysqld1] group for 5.7.9 and the [mysqld2] group for 8.0.25. For example, you can set up C:\my.cnf in the following manner:[4]

```
# options for mysqld1 service
[mysqld1]
basedir = C:/mysql-5.7.9
port = 3307
```

---

[4] https://dev.mysql.com/doc/refman/8.0/en/multiple-windows-services.html, MySQL

```
enable-named-pipe
socket = mypipe1

# options for mysqld2 service
[mysqld2]
basedir = C:/mysql-8.0.25
port = 3308
enable-named-pipe
socket = mypipe2
```

In order to install the services as follows, you have to use the full server path names to ensure that Windows registers the correct executable program for each service:[5]

```
C:\> C:\mysql-5.7.9\bin\mysqld
--install mysqld1
C:\> C:\mysql-8.0.25\bin\mysqld
--install mysqld2
```

To start the services, you can use the services manager, or NET START or SC START with the appropriate service names:

```
C:\> SC START mysqld1
C:\> SC START mysqld2
```

And to stop the services, apply the services manager, or use NET STOP or SC STOP with the appropriate service names:

```
C:\> SC STOP mysqld1
C:\> SC STOP mysqld2
```

---

[5] https://dev.mysql.com/doc/refman/8.0/en/multiple-windows-services.html, MySQL

- **Method 2:** Designate options for each server in separate files and use --defaults-file when you install the services to command each server what file to use. In this case, each file should list options using a [mysqld] group.

With this approach, to specify options for the 5.7.9 mysqld, create a file C:\my-opts1.cnf that looks like this:

```
[mysqld]
basedir = C:/mysql-5.7.9
port = 3307
enable-named-pipe
socket = mypipe1
```

For the 8.0.25 mysqld, create a file C:\my-opts2.cnf that looks like this:

```
[mysqld]
basedir = C:/mysql-8.0.25
port = 3308
enable-named-pipe
socket = mypipe2
```

You can then install the services as follows:

```
C:\> C:\mysql-5.7.9\bin\mysqld --install
mysqld1
          --defaults-file=C:\my-opts1.cnf
C:\> C:\mysql-8.0.25\bin\mysqld --install
mysqld2
          --defaults-file=C:\my-opts2.cnf
```

When you install a MySQL server as a service and apply a --defaults-file option, the service name must precede the option. After installing the services, make sure to start and stop them the same way as in the first method example.

Similarly, in order to remove multiple services, use SC DELETE mysqld_service_name for each one. Or as an alternative, use mysqld --remove for each one, identifying a service name following the --remove option. If the service name is the default, you can ignore it when using mysqld --remove.

### Running Multiple MySQL Instances on Unix

For MySQL installation using an RPM distribution, server startup and shutdown is regulated by systemd on several Linux platforms. On these platforms, mysqld_safe is not installed because it is not considered necessary.

One way to run multiple MySQL instances on Unix is to combine different servers with different default TCP/IP ports and Unix socket files so that each one listens to different network interfaces. Compiling in different base directories for each installation also happens automatically in a separate, compiled-in data directory, log file, and PID file location for each server.

To demonstrate, imagine that an existing 5.7 server is configured for the default TCP/IP port number (4406) and Unix socket file (/tmp/mysql.sock). To configure a new 8.0.25 server to have different operating parameters, try the following CMake command:

```
shell> cmake . -DMYSQL_TCP_
PORT=port_number \
            -DMYSQL_UNIX_ADDR=file_name \
            -DCMAKE_INSTALL_PREFIX=/usr/
local/mysql-8.0.25
```

Here, port_number and file_name should be different from the default TCP/IP port number and Unix socket file pathname, and the CMAKE_INSTALL_PREFIX value should explicitly state an installation directory different from the one under which the existing MySQL installation is placed.

In case you have a MySQL server listening on a given port number, you can include the following command to see what operating parameters it is using for several important configurable variables, including the base directory and Unix socket file name:

```
shell> mysqladmin --host=host_name
--port=port_number variables
```

With the information presented by that command, you can find out what option values not to use when setting up an additional server.

In addition, if you specify localhost as the hostname, mysqladmin defaults to using a Unix socket file rather than TCP/IP. To explicitly regulate the transport protocol, attempt the --protocol={TCP|SOCKET|PIPE|MEMORY} option.

There is no need to combine a whole new MySQL server just to start with a different Unix socket file and TCP/IP port number. You can potentially use the same server binary and start each invocation of it with different parameter values at runtime. One way to accomplish it would be by using command-line options:

```
shell> mysqld_safe --socket=file_name
--port=port_number
```

And to start a second server, provide different --socket and --port option values, and pass a --datadir=dir_name option to mysqld_safe so that the server applies a different data directory.

As an alternative, you can put the options for each server in a different option file, then start each server using a --defaults-file option that identifies the path to the suitable option file. To illustrate with an example, if the option files for two server instances are named /usr/local/MySQL/my.cnf and /usr/local/MySQL/my.cnf2, start the servers with this command:[6]

```
shell> mysqld_safe --defaults-file=/usr/
local/mysql/my.cnf
shell> mysqld_safe --defaults-file=/usr/
local/mysql/my.cnf2
```

You can also achieve a similar effect using environment variables that set the Unix socket file name and TCP/IP port number:[7]

```
shell> MYSQL_UNIX_PORT=/tmp/mysqld-new.sock
shell> MYSQL_TCP_PORT=3307
shell> export MYSQL_UNIX_PORT
MYSQL_TCP_PORT
shell> bin/mysqld --initialize --user=mysql
shell> mysqld_safe --datadir=/path/to/
datadir &
```

---

[6] https://dev.mysql.com/doc/refman/8.0/en/multiple-windows-services.html, MySQL

[7] https://dev.mysql.com/doc/refman/8.0/en/multiple-windows-services.html, MySQL

That would probably be the quickest way of starting a second server for testing purposes. The good thing about this approach is that the environment variable settings apply to any user programs that you activate from the same shell. Therefore, connections for those users are automatically directed to the second server.

## CREATING AND MANAGING USERS AND ROLES

User management and security control are two areas that can quickly become multiplex as the number of users and database entities increases. Managing many different privileges on different database objects, making sure users that have the same responsibilities have the same level of access, monitoring, and inspecting access all become more complicated with time.

To help with this, MySQL came up with a concept called "roles" that permits you to group sets of privileges under a given name, allowing you to assign and edit overarching settings. In this section, we shall go through roles that work within MySQL and learn how to use them to make it easier to regulate data access for all users. Each row in the MySQL.user table is identified by a user and host tuple. This tuple stands for the authorization ID. A client can authenticate with an authorization ID and a password. The ID is then referred to as a user or user name. Here, before going any further, let's go through some of the main definitions:

- **Privileges ID:** A privilege ID could be viewed as a token that is granted to an authorization ID. A privilege can either be effective or not effective. An effective privilege is the one used in a session to assess if a particular operation is permitted or not.

- **Roles:** A role is an authorization ID that can be assigned to another authorization ID by establishing a directed edge between them in the role graph where every vertex is a unique authorization ID. When the effective privilege is estimated, all connected roles are assessed according to their edge direction and corresponding granted privileges they possess.

- **Active roles:** A role can either be active or inactive. Active roles are located in a thread-local list which exists only for the lifetime of a user session. Granted roles can be turned into active by (1) a SET ROLE statement, (2) after authentication if the role is a default role, and (3) after authentication if the global variable opt_always_activate_roles_on_login is set to true.

- **Default roles:** Each authorization ID has a list of default roles. Default roles belonging to an authorization ID are turned into active roles after authentication. If the list of default roles is empty, then no roles are made active after authentication unless the user sets a SET ROLE statement.

- **Mandatory roles:** A mandatory role is an authorization ID that is granted to every other authorization ID which has authenticated, regardless if this role has been previously granted or not. Mandatory roles are designated in a global variable. It is not required that the specified list maps to any existing authorization ID, but if there is no previous record of authorization ID, then no mandatory role can be granted. Mandatory roles are processed similarly to any other granted role when the effective privilege of an authorization ID needs to be assessed.

A user account can be permitted roles, which grants to the account the privileges connected to each role. This enables the assignment of privilege sets as a convenient alternative to granting individual privileges, both for structuring desired privilege assignments and realizing them.

The following list sums up role-management capacities provided by MySQL:[8]

- CREATE ROLE and DROP ROLE to create and delete roles.

- GRANT and REVOKE assign privileges and revoke privileges from accounts and roles.

- SHOW GRANTS demonstrates privilege and role assignments for accounts and roles.

---

[8] https://dev.mysql.com/doc/refman/8.0/en/roles.html, MySQL

- SET DEFAULT ROLE identifies which account roles are active by default.

- SET ROLE changes the active roles within the current session.

- The CURRENT_ROLE() function displays the active roles within the current session.

- The mandatory_roles and activate_all_roles_on_login system variables enable determining mandatory roles and automatic activation of granted roles when users log in to the server.

## Creating Roles and Granting Privileges to Them

It potentially could happen so that a database associated with the application, can have multiple accounts for developers who create and maintain the application, and separate accounts only for users who interact with it. Developers typically require full access to the database while users need only read access, or read/write access.

To avoid granting privileges individually to many user accounts, you can create roles as names for the required privilege sets. This makes it easy to grant the privileges to user accounts, by granting the appropriate roles.

To create the roles, insert the CREATE ROLE statement:

```
CREATE ROLE 'app_developer', 'app_read',
'app_write';
```

Role names are similar to user account names in the way how both consist of a user part and host part in 'user_name'@'host_name' manner. The host part, if skipped, defaults to '%'. The user and host parts can stay unquoted unless they hold special characters such as - or %. However, unlike account names, the user part of role names cannot be left blank.

In order to assign privileges to the roles, you should execute GRANT statement using the same syntax as for assigning privileges to user accounts:[9]

```
GRANT ALL ON app_db.* TO 'app_developer';
GRANT SELECT ON app_db.* TO 'app_read';
GRANT INSERT, UPDATE, DELETE ON app_db.*
TO 'app_write';
```

Now let's imagine that you initially require one developer account, two user accounts that need read-only access, and one user account that needs read/write access. You can accomplish that by using CREATE USER to create these accounts:

```
CREATE USER 'dev1'@'localhost' IDENTIFIED
BY 'dev1pass';
CREATE USER 'read_user1'@'localhost'
IDENTIFIED BY 'read_user1pass';
CREATE USER 'read_user2'@'localhost'
IDENTIFIED BY 'read_user2pass';
CREATE USER 'rw_user1'@'localhost'
IDENTIFIED BY 'rw_user1pass';
```

To assign each user account its appropriate privileges, you can use GRANT statements of the same format as

---

[9] https://dev.mysql.com/doc/refman/8.0/en/roles.html, MySQL

mentioned above, but that requires enumerating individual privileges for each user. Instead, try using an alternative GRANT syntax that allows granting roles rather than privileges:[10]

```
GRANT 'app_developer' TO
'dev1'@'localhost';
GRANT 'app_read' TO 'read_
user1'@'localhost',
'read_user2'@''localhost';
GRANT 'app_read', 'app_write' TO
'rw_user1'@'localhost';
```

The GRANT syntax for granting roles to an account is not the same as the syntax for granting privileges. There is an ON clause to assign privileges, whereas there is no ON clause to assign roles. And because the syntaxes are different, you cannot combine assigning privileges and roles in the same statement.

Typically, a role when created is locked, has no password, and is designated with the default authentication plugin. At the same time, these role attributes can be altered later with the ALTER USER statement, by users who hold the global CREATE USER privilege.

While locked, a role cannot be applied to authenticate to the server. Only once unlocked, it can be used to authenticate. This is due to the fact that roles and users are both authorization identifiers with much in common and little to distinguish them.

---

[10] https://dev.mysql.com/doc/refman/8.0/en/roles.html, MySQL

## Defining Mandatory Roles

It is possible to define roles as mandatory by naming them in the value of the mandatory_roles system variable. The server presumes a mandatory role is granted to all users so that it need not be granted separately to any account. To identify mandatory roles at server startup, define mandatory_roles in your server my.cnf file:

```
[mysqld]
mandatory_roles='role1,role2@
localhost,r3@%.example.com'
```

To establish and maintain mandatory_roles at runtime, you should use the following statement:[11]

```
SET PERSIST mandatory_roles = 'role1,role2@
localhost,r3@%.example.com';
```

SET PERSIST sets the value for the running MySQL instance. It also saves the value, causing it to transfer to subsequent server restarts. To modify the value for the running MySQL instance without having it carry over to subsequent restarts, insert the GLOBAL keyword rather than PERSIST.

Setting mandatory_roles requires the ROLE_ADMIN privilege, in addition to the SYSTEM_VARIABLES_ ADMIN privilege normally applied to set a global system variable.

Mandatory roles, similar to granted roles, do not produce results until activated. At login time, role activation

---

[11] https://dev.mysql.com/doc/refman/8.0/en/roles.html, MySQL

takes place for all granted roles if the activate_all_roles_ on_login system variable is enabled, or for roles that are set as default roles. You can apply the SET ROLE command at runtime to complete activation. However, roles named in the value of mandatory_roles cannot be revoked with REVOKE or dropped with DROP ROLE or DROP USER.

In order to prevent sessions from being made system sessions by default, a role that has the SYSTEM_USER privilege cannot be included in the value of the mandatory_roles system variable for the following reasons:[12]

- If mandatory_roles is assigned a role at startup that has the SYSTEM_USER privilege, the server drops a message to the error log and exits.

- If mandatory_roles is assigned a role at runtime that has the SYSTEM_USER privilege, an error occurs and the mandatory_roles value remains unmodified.

- If a role named in mandatory_roles is not included in the MySQL.user system table, the role is not granted to users. If the server attempts role activation for a user, it does not take the nonexistent role as mandatory and writes a warning to the error log. If the role is created later and thus becomes valid, FLUSH PRIVILEGES may be necessary to cause the server to take it as mandatory.

---

[12] https://dev.mysql.com/doc/refman/8.0/en/account-categories.html, MySQL

## Checking Role Privileges

In order to check and confirm the privileges assigned to an account, you should use SHOW GRANTS variable in the following format:

```
mysql> SHOW GRANTS FOR 'dev1'@'localhost';
Grants for dev1@localhost
GRANT USAGE ON *.* TO 'dev1'@'localhost'
GRANT 'app_developer'@'%' TO
'dev1'@'localhost'
```

At the same time, the variable will show each granted role without "expanding" it to the privileges the role represents. To display role privileges as well, you need to include a USING clause naming the granted roles for which to display privileges:

```
mysql> SHOW GRANTS FOR 'dev1'@'localhost'
USING 'app_developer';
Grants for dev1@localhost
GRANT USAGE ON *.* TO 'dev1'@'localhost'
GRANT ALL PRIVILEGES ON 'app_db'.* TO
'dev1'@'localhost'
GRANT 'app_developer'@'%' TO
'dev1'@'localhost'
```

## Activating Roles

Roles granted to a user account can be treated as active or inactive within account sessions. If a granted role is active within a session, its privileges are included as well; otherwise, they are not. If might want to see for yourself which roles are active within the current session, use the CURRENT_ROLE() function for that purpose.

By default, granting a role to an account or naming it in the mandatory_roles system variable value does not automatically make the role active within account sessions. For instance, because thus far in the preceding discussion no rw_user1 roles have been activated, if you connect to the server as rw_user1 and insert the CURRENT_ROLE() function, the result will be NONE (meaning no active roles):

```
mysql> SELECT CURRENT_ROLE();
CURRENT_ROLE()
NONE
```

To correctly identify which roles should become active each time a user links to the server and authenticates, you should apply SET DEFAULT ROLE. To set the default to all designated roles for each account created earlier, you should use the following statement:

```
SET DEFAULT ROLE ALL TO
'dev1'@'localhost',
'read_user1'@'localhost',
'read_user2'@'localhost',
'rw_user1'@'localhost';
```

Now if you try and connect as rw_user1, the initial value of CURRENT_ROLE() will display the new default role assignments:

```
mysql> SELECT CURRENT_ROLE();
CURRENT_ROLE()
'app_read'@'%','app_write'@'%'
```

And in case you want to set all explicitly granted and mandatory roles to be automatically activated once you connect to the server, just enable the activate_all_roles_ on_login system variable because, by default, this option is disabled.

### Revoking Roles or Role Privileges

Just as roles can be granted to an account, they can also be revoked from an account via REVOKE role FROM user command. Yet keep in mind that roles named in the mandatory_roles system variable value cannot be revoked.

REVOKE can be applied to a role to transform the privileges granted to it. This impacts not only the role itself but any account granted that role. Let's say you need to temporarily make all application users read-only. For that, use REVOKE to revoke the modification privileges from the app_write role: REVOKE INSERT, UPDATE, DELETE ON app_db.* FROM 'app_write';

As it proceeds, that leaves the role with no privileges at all, as can be seen using SHOW GRANTS that is used to demonstrate that this statement can be used with roles, not just users:

```
mysql> SHOW GRANTS FOR 'app_write';
Grants for app_write@%
GRANT USAGE ON *.* TO 'app_write'@'%'
```

Due to the fact that revoking privileges from a role transform the privileges for any user who is assigned the modified role, rw_user1 now has no table modification privileges (meaning INSERT, UPDATE, and DELETE are no longer available):

```
mysql> SHOW GRANTS FOR
'rw_user1'@'localhost'
USING 'app_read', 'app_write';
Grants for rw_user1@localhost
GRANT USAGE ON *.* TO
'rw_user1'@'localhost'
GRANT SELECT ON 'app_db'.* TO
'rw_user1'@'localhost'
GRANT 'app_read'@'%','app_write'@'%' TO
'rw_user1'@'localhost'
```

As a result, the rw_user1 read/write user has become a read-only user. This is also true for any other accounts that are granted the app_write role, demonstrating how the use of roles makes it unnecessary to modify privileges for individual accounts.

And in case you would need to restore modification privileges to the role, you can achieve that by simply re-granting them: GRANT INSERT, UPDATE, DELETE ON app_db.* TO 'app_write'; With that, rw_user1 again will have modification privileges, similar to any other accounts granted the app_write role.

And to drop the roles, just apply DROP ROLE: DROP ROLE 'app_read', 'app_write';

This function revokes a role from every account to which it was granted. Yet roles named in the mandatory_roles system variable value cannot be dropped.

## User and Role Interchangeability

As has been previously, SHOW GRANTS can be used to display grants for both user accounts and roles, where accounts and roles are typically used interchangeably.

A significant difference between roles and users is that CREATE ROLE creates an authorization identifier that is locked by default, whereas CREATE USER creates an authorization identifier that is unlocked by default. However, the distinction is not immutable because a user with suitable privileges can lock or unlock roles or users after they have been created.

Thus, in case a DBA has a preference that a specific authorization identifier must be a role, a name scheme can be applied to execute this intention. For instance, you could use a r_ prefix for all authorization identifiers that you want to transform into roles and nothing else.

Another difference between roles and users lies in the privileges that are used for managing them:

The CREATE ROLE and DROP ROLE privileges enable only use of the CREATE ROLE and DROP ROLE statements, respectively.

The CREATE USER privilege activates the use of the ALTER USER, CREATE ROLE, CREATE USER, DROP ROLE, DROP USER, RENAME USER, and REVOKE ALL PRIVILEGES statements. Therefore, it is safe to say that the CREATE ROLE and DROP ROLE privileges are not as dynamic as CREATE USER and may be granted to users who should only be allowed to create and drop roles, and not perform more general account handling.

With reference to the interchangeability of users and roles, you can view a user account like a role and grant that account to another user or a role. The idea is to grant the account's privileges and roles to the other user or role. Normally, if a developer leaves the project, it becomes necessary to transfer the privileges to another user, or perhaps multiple users if development activities have increased. You can complete this task in the following way:

Without using roles: opting for changing the account password so the original developer cannot use it, and have a new developer use the account instead:

```
ALTER USER 'old_app_dev'@'localhost'
IDENTIFIED BY 'new_password';
```

Using roles: Choosing to simply lock the account to prevent anyone from connecting to the server:

```
ALTER USER 'old_app_dev'@'localhost'
ACCOUNT LOCK;
```

As an alternative, you can also treat the account as a role. Meaning that for each developer you create a new account and grant to it the original developer account via:

```
CREATE USER 'new_app_dev1'@'localhost'
IDENTIFIED BY 'new_password';
GRANT 'old_app_dev'@'localhost' TO
'new_app_dev1'@'localhost';
```

Using roles to diversify privileges in your MySQL databases can help disentangle the management structure and complexity of your access security system. It is easier to make sure that users with the same responsibilities have the same privileges using roles than it is to distribute many different privileges directly.

Similarly, roles let you be explicit about the overall aim behind your privilege granting. Rather than granting large numbers of privileges to accounts without any commentary, carefully selected role names can assist in distinguishing between different levels of access. By taking the time to create and operate roles, your capacity to manage user access to different sections of your data will look more elementary in the long run.

## IMPORTING AND EXPORTING DATABASE

It is a well-known fact that your network applications depend upon databases. In fact, much of what you work with depends upon a database or two. Due to that, it is highly recommended to not only have backups of those databases but to also learn how to export and import them from either machine or database server. Importing and exporting databases should not be feared but rather considered as a regular task in software development. You can use data dumps to back up and data restoration as well as migration of data to a new server or development environment.

In this section, we shall see how you can work with database dumps in MySQL or MariaDB (the most popular option). Specifically, we will review step by step approach on how to export a database and then import that same database from the dump file.

As basic prerequisites to import or export a MySQL or MariaDB database, you would require:

- A virtual machine with a non-root sudo user

- MySQL or MariaDB installed

- A sample database created in your database server

### Exporting a MySQL or MariaDB Database

The mysqldump console is mostly used to export databases to SQL text files. This utility makes it easier for you to move or transfer databases. You would also need your database's name and credentials for an account whose privileges permit at least full read-only access to the database.

To activate mysqldump to export your database insert the following command:

```
mysqldump -u username -p database_name >
data-dump.sql
```

- username stands for the standard username you can log in to the database with.

- database_name is the name of the database you are going to export.

- data-dump.sql is the file in the current directory that stores the output/.

This command will not produce any substantial visual output, but you can examine the contents of data-dump.sql to check if it is a legitimate SQL dump file. For that, run the following command:

```
head -n 5 data-dump.sql
```

The headline of the file should look similar to this, showing a MySQL dump for a database named database_name:

-- MySQL dump 10.13 Distrib 5.7.16, for Linux (x86_64)

-- Host: localhost   Database: database_name

-- Server version      5.7.16-0ubuntu0.18.04.1

In case any errors occur during the export process, mysql-dump will display them to you on the screen.

### Importing a MySQL or MariaDB Database

To import an existing dump file into MySQL or MariaDB, you will need to create a new database. This database will contain the imported data.

First, start by logging into MySQL as root or another user with enough privileges to create new databases:

```
MySQL -u root -p
```

This particular command will bring you into the MySQL shell prompt. Next, create a new database with the following command. Just to demonstrate, the new database would be named new_database:

```
CREATE DATABASE new_database;
```

You will then be able to see this output confirming the database creation:

- Output
  Query OK, 1 row affected (0.00 sec)

Once you see that, you can exit the MySQL shell by pressing CTRL+D. From the normal command line, you can import the dump file with the following command:

```
MySQL -u username -p new_database < data-
dump.sql
```

- username stands for the standard username you can log in to the database with.

- new database is the name of the freshly created database.

- data-dump.sql is the data dump file to be imported, placed in the current directory.

If the command runs successfully, it should not produce any output. But in case any errors occur during the process, MySQL will display them to the terminal instead. To check if the import was successful, log in to the MySQL shell and inspect the data. You can select the new database with USE new_database and then use SHOW TABLES; or a similar command to look at some of the data.

With that, there is all to start migrating a database from one MySQL server to another. The only problem could be if you are still working with a much older MySQL database, and there are inconsistencies between how that older database handled tables and/or data, versus how the newer MariaDB server works with tables and/or data. To prevent that, make sure you are not running an old utility for every procedure to work just fine in the end.

# CHAPTER 6

# Backing Up and Restoring MySQL Data

## IN THIS CHAPTER

➤ Finding out how to create a backup file in MySQL

➤ Restoring MySQL data files

➤ Exploring configurations of CSV format data

DOI: 10.1201/9781003229629-6

Backup and restoration of MySQL databases play a crucial role in a production environment. This chapter will focus on the most common tools for generating backups in several formats or restoring MySQL databases.

## CREATING A BACKUP FILE

It is essential to back up your databases so that you can recover your data and be up and running again in case issues occur, such as hardware crashes, system failures, or something as simple as users deleting data by mistake. Backups are also important as a safeguard before upgrading a MySQL installation, and they can be utilized to transfer a MySQL installation to another system or to organize replica servers.

For that, MySQL offers a variety of backup schemes from which you can select the methods that suit particular requirements for your installation. Let's see what types and characteristics are there.

### Physical and Logical Backups

Physical backups consist of raw files of the directories and files that are used to cache database loads. This particular type of backup is perfect for larger, main databases that need to be recovered fast in case problems occur.

Logical backups, on the other hand, save data illustrated as logical database structure (CREATE DATABASE, CREATE TABLE statements) and content (INSERT statements or delimited-text files). This type of backup is most useful for smaller amounts of data where you need to modify the data values or table structure or recreate the data on a different machine.

Physical backup methods have the following key characteristics:

- The backup holds exact copies of database directories and files. Usually, this is a copy of all or specific bits of the MySQL data directory.

- Physical backup methods are typically faster than logical due to the fact that they process only file copying without conversion.

- Output produced is more compact in size and quantity than for logical backup.

Because backup speed and concentration are important for active and important databases, the MySQL Enterprise Backup product completes physical backups. Backup and restoration level ranges from the entire data directory down to the level of separate files. It also very much depends on the individual storage engine characteristics. For instance, InnoDB tables can each be in a separate file or share data storage with other InnoDB tables; while each MyISAM table can correspond uniquely only to a set of files.

In addition to databases, the backup can involve any other related files such as log or configuration files. Backups are also portable to other machines that have identical or similar hardware characteristics. Backups can be performed while the MySQL server is not running. And if the server is running, you have to perform appropriate locking so that the server does not modify database contents during the backup. Luckily, MySQL Enterprise Backup does this locking automatically for tables that require it.

Physical backup tools include the mysqlbackup of MySQL Enterprise Backup for InnoDB or any other tables or file system-level commands (such as cp, SCP, tar, rsync) for MyISAM tables. Moreover, MySQL Enterprise Backup applies ndb_restore to restore NDB tables and copies files at the file system level back to their original locations with file system commands.

Logical backup methods are distinguished by the following characteristics:[1]

- The backup is done by requesting the MySQL server to obtain database structure and content information.

- Backup is slower than physical methods because the server has to access database information and convert it to logical format. When the output is written on the client-side, the server should also send it to the backup program.

- Output is larger than for physical backup, especially when saved in text format.

- Backup and restore granularity is available at the server level (all databases), database level (all tables in a particular database), or table level. This is true regardless of the storage engine.

- The backup does not include log or configuration files, or other database-related files that are not part of databases.

---

[1] https://dev.mysql.com/doc/mysql-backup-excerpt/8.0/en/backup-types. html, MySQL

- Backups stored in logical format are machine-independent and highly portable.

- Logical backups are completed with the MySQL server running. The server is not taken offline.

- Logical backup tools include the mysqldump program and the SELECT ... INTO OUTFILE statement. These operate for any storage engine, even MEMORY.

- To restore logical backups, SQL-format dump files can be processed using the MySQL client. To load delimited-text files, use the LOAD DATA statement or the mysqlimport client.

## Online and Offline Backups

Online backups are processed while the MySQL server is running so that the database information can be delivered from the server. Offline backups happen when the server is stopped. This difference can also be described as "hot" versus "cold" backups; a "warm" backup is one where the server keeps running but locked against editing data while you access database files externally.

Online backup methods have these distinct characteristics:

- The backup is less forward to other clients, which can connect to the MySQL server during the backup and may be able to access data depending on what operations they want to perform.

- You need to make sure you impose appropriate locking so that data modifications cannot compromise backup integrity. The MySQL Enterprise Backup product does such locking automatically.

Offline backup methods characteristics are the following:

- Clients can be affected adversely because the server is unavailable during backup. For that reason, such backups are often taken from a replica server that can be taken offline without compromising availability.

- The backup procedure is more straightforward because there is not a chance of interference from the client-side.

A similar distinction between online and offline applies to recovery operations as well. However, it is more likely for clients to be affected by online recovery than for online backup because recovery requires stronger locking. During backup, clients might be able to read data while it is being backed up. Recovery modifies data and disables reading it, so clients must be prevented from accessing data while it is being restored.

## Local and Remote Backups

A local backup is completed on the same host where the MySQL server runs, whereas a remote backup is performed from a different host. For some types of backups, the backup can be activated from a remote host even if the output is written locally on the server host.

mysqldump is a great tool to connect to local or remote servers. For SQL output (CREATE and INSERT statements), local or remote dumps can be done and produce output on the client. For delimited-text output (with the --tab option), data files are created on the server host.

Nevertheless, SELECT … INTO OUTFILE can be activated from a local or remote client host, but the output file is created on the server host. Physical backup methods normally are initiated locally on the MySQL server host so that the server can be taken offline, although the location for copied files could be remote.

## Snapshot Backups

Some file system executions enable "snapshots" function to be activated. These provide logical copies of the file system at any point in time, without having to request a physical copy of the entire file system. The backup execution may use the copy-on-write method so that only a section of the file system modified after the snapshot time needs to be copied. However, MySQL itself does not have the capacity for taking file system snapshots. It is only available through third-party solutions such as Veritas, LVM, or ZFS.

## Full and Incremental Backups

A full backup includes all data administered by a MySQL server. An incremental backup consists of the modifications made to the data during a given time span (from one point in time to another). MySQL has different methods to complete full backups as those described earlier in this chapter. Incremental backups are made available by enabling the server's binary log, which the server applies to document any data changes.

## Full and Point-in-Time (Incremental) Recovery

A full recovery can bring back all data from a full backup. This restores the server instance to the condition that it had when the backup was made. If that state is not completely current, a full recovery can be followed by several instances of incremental backups made since the full backup, to bring the server to a re-equipped state.

Incremental recovery is the recovery of changes made during a specific time frame. This is also called point-in-time recovery because it turns a server's state current up to a certain time. Point-in-time recovery is based on the binary log and typically follows a full recovery from the backup files that restores the server to its state when the backup was made. Then the data changes written in the binary log files are utilized as incremental recovery to recover data modifications and bring the server up to the designated point in time.

In addition, you can make use of backup scheduling to automate any planned backup procedures. Compression of backup output decreased space requirements, and encryption of the output provides better security against undesired access of backed-up data. However, MySQL itself does not have these capacities on its own. The MySQL Enterprise Backup product can compress InnoDB backups, and compression or encryption of backup output can be achieved using file system utilities. As an alternative, you can always seek other third-party solutions.

With that, let's take a look at some other standard methods for making backups.

## Making a Hot Backup with MySQL Enterprise Backup

Users of MySQL Enterprise Edition can apply the product to complete physical backups of entire instances, selected databases, and tables. This product also has features for incremental and compressed backups. Backing up the physical database files makes restore much faster than logical techniques such as the mysqldump command. Yet tables from other storage engines are copied using a warm backup mechanism.

## Making Backups with mysqldump

The mysqldump program is great for backing up all kinds of tables. Even for InnoDB tables, it is possible to perform an online backup that takes no locks on tables using the --single-transaction option of mysqldump.

## Making Backups by Copying Table Files

For storage engines that represent each table using its own files, tables can be backed up by copying those files. For instance, MyISAM tables are saved as files, so it is easy to complete a backup by copying files (*.frm, *.MYD, and *.MYI files). To achieve a consistent backup, you need to stop the server or lock and flush the relevant tables: FLUSH TABLES tbl_list WITH READ LOCK;

This would enable other clients to continue to request the tables while you are making a copy of the files in the database directory. The flush is necessary to ensure that all active index pages are placed to disk before you activate the backup.

You can also complete a binary backup just by copying all table files, as long as the server is not updating anything. But at the same time, that table file copying methods do not operate if your database has InnoDB tables in it. Also, even if the server is not actively updating data, InnoDB may still have edited data located in memory and not transferred to disk.

## Making Delimited-Text File Backups

To create a text file holding a table's data, you can use SELECT * INTO OUTFILE 'file_name' FROM tbl_name. The file is produced on the MySQL server host, not the client host. For this statement, the output file cannot already exist because letting files be overwritten is defined as a major security risk. This method applies to any kind of data file but saves only table data, not the table structure.

An alternative way to create text data files along with files containing CREATE TABLE statements for the backed-up tables is to apply mysqldump with the --tab option. In order to reload a delimited-text data file, use LOAD DATA or mysqlimport.

## Making Incremental Backups by Enabling the Binary Log

MySQL supports incremental backups. But in order to activate the option, you should start the server with the --log-bin option to enable binary logging. The binary log files provide you with the system methods you need to replicate changes to the database that are made subsequent to the point at which you completed a backup. If you want to make an incremental backup containing all changes that happened since the last full or incremental backup, you should rotate the binary log by using FLUSH LOGS. After that, you need to copy to the backup location all binary logs which range from one of the moments of the last full or incremental backup to the last but one. These binary logs represent the incremental backup, and the next time you do a full backup, you should also rotate the binary log using FLUSH LOGS or mysqldump --flush-logs.

## Making Backups Using Replicas

If you face performance problems with your source server while making backups, one way that can help is to set up replication and complete backups on the replica rather than on the source.

When you are backing up a replica server, you should back up its source info and relay log info repositories when you back up the replica's databases, regardless of the backup type you follow. These information files are always needed to resume replication after you restore the replica's data. If your replica is replicating LOAD DATA statements, you should also back up any SQL_LOAD-* files that are located in the directory that the replica uses for this purpose. The replica needs these files to complete replication of any interrupted LOAD DATA operations. The location of this directory is the value of the slave_load_tmpdir system variable. If the server was not started with that variable set, the directory location is the value of the tmpdir system variable.

In addition, when recovering corrupt tables, it is most efficient to recover them using REPAIR TABLE or myisamchk -r options first.

## Making Backups Using a File System Snapshot

If you are a Veritas file system user, you can complete a backup with a system snapshot in the following manner:

- From a client program, go to execute FLUSH TABLES WITH READ LOCK

- From another shell, select to execute Mount vxfs Snapshot

- From the first client, click on UNLOCK TABLES

- Copy files from the snapshot

- And at last, unmount the snapshot

*Establishing a Backup Habit*

To bring maximum benefits, backups must be scheduled regularly. A full backup (a snapshot of the data at a point in time) can be done in MySQL with several utilities. For example, MySQL Enterprise Backup can perform a physical backup of an entire instance, with optimizations to minimize failure and avoid disruption when backing up InnoDB data files; in addition, mysqldump can provide online logical backup.

Let's imagine that we need to perform a full backup of all our InnoDB tables in all databases using the following command on Friday at 1 p.m., when load is low:

```
shell> mysqldump --all-databases --master-
data --single-transaction >
backup_friday_1_PM.sql
```

The produced .sql file by mysqldump holds a set of SQL INSERT statements that can later be used to reload the dumped tables.

This backup operation results in a global read lock on all tables at the beginning of the dump (using FLUSH TABLES WITH READ LOCK). Thus, once this lock has been acquired, the binary log coordinates are read, and the lock is released. If long updating statements are running when the FLUSH statement is produced, the backup operation may be paused until those statements finish. After that, the dump becomes lock-free and does not affect reads and writes on the tables.

It was mentioned earlier that the tables to back up are InnoDB tables, so --single-transaction uses a consistent read and guarantees that data seen by mysqldump does not change. But if the backup operation includes nontransactional tables, consistency requires that they do not change during the backup. For instance, for the MyISAM tables in the MySQL database, there must be no administrative modifications to MySQL accounts during the backup.

Even though full backups are necessary, it is not always convenient to process them. They produce large backup files and take a substantial amount of time to generate. They are not preferred in the sense that each set of full backup includes all data, even that part that has not changed since the previous full backup. It is therefore more efficient to complete an initial full backup, and then to make incremental backups. The incremental backups are much smaller and take fewer resources to produce. But at the same time, during the recovery period, you cannot restore your data just by reloading the full backup. You must also process the incremental backups to recover the incremental changes.

In order to make incremental backups, we need to save the incremental changes. In MySQL, these changes are demonstrated in the binary log, so the MySQL server should always be started with the --log-bin option to enable that log. With binary logging enabled, the server copies each data change into a file while it updates data. And each time it restarts, the MySQL server creates a new binary log file using the next number in the sequence. While the server is running, you can also regulate it to shut the current binary log file and begin a new one manually by inserting a FLUSH LOGS SQL statement or with a mysqladmin flush-logs command. mysqldump also has an option to flush the logs at the list of all MySQL binary logs in the directory.

The MySQL binary logs are important for recovery because they shape the set of incremental backups. If you make sure to flush the logs when you make your full backup, the binary log files created afterward hold all the data changes added since the backup. Let's try to modify the previous mysqldump command to see that it flushes the MySQL binary logs at the moment of the full backup, and so that the dump file contains the name of the new current binary log:

```
shell> mysqldump --single-transaction
--flush-logs --master-data=2\
        --all-databases >
backup_friday_1_PM.sql
```

After implementing this command, the data directory contains a new binary log file, gbichot2-bin.000007, because the --flush-logs option causes the server to flush its logs. The --master-data option causes mysqldump to write binary log information to its output, so the resulting .sql dump file includes these lines:

--Position to start replication or point-in-time recovery from the current time or state

--CHANGE MASTER TO MASTER_LOG_FILE='gbichot2-bin.000007',MASTER_LOG_POS=4;

Because the mysqldump command made a full backup, those lines mean two things:

> The dump file contains all changes made before any changes written to the gbichot2-bin.000007 binary log file or higher. And that all data changes logged after the backup are not included in the dump file, but are present in the gbichot2-bin.000007 binary log file or higher.

Now let's try and create an incremental backup by flushing the logs to begin a new binary log file on Saturday at 1 p.m. To illustrate, executing a mysqladmin flush-logs command creates gbichot2-bin.000008. All changes between the Friday 1 p.m. full backup and Saturday 1 p.m. are in the gbichot2-bin.000007 files. This incremental backup is crucial, so it is recommended to copy it to a safe place such as tape or DVD. On Sunday at 1 p.m., implement another mysqladmin flush-logs command. All changes between Saturday 1 p.m. and Sunday 1 p.m. will be located at the gbichot2-bin.000008 file.

It is known that the MySQL binary logs take up most of the disk space. Therefore, in order to free up some space, you can extract them from time to time. One way to do this is by deleting the binary logs that are no longer necessary during the full backup:

```
shell> mysqldump --single-transaction
--flush-logs --master-data=2 \
          --all-databases --delete-master-
logs > backup_sunday_1_PM.sql
```

At the same time, removing the MySQL binary logs with mysqldump --delete-master-logs can be dangerous if your server is a replication source server because replica servers might not yet fully have regulated the contents of the binary log.

Also note that in case of an operating system failure or power crush, the database itself can fully recover all the data. But to make sure that it can be done well, observe the following recommendations:[2]

- Always run the MySQL server with the --log-bin option, or even --log-bin=log_name, where the log file name is located on some safe media different from the drive on which the data directory is located. If you have such safe media, this technique can also be good for disk load balancing (which impacts the overall performance).

- Do not forget about the periodic full backups, using the mysqldump command that facilitates an online, non-blocking backup.

- Make periodic incremental backups by flushing the logs with FLUSH LOGS or mysqladmin flush-logs.

From now we shall examine how to use mysqldump to produce dump files, and how to reload them. To start with, a dump file can be used in several ways:

- As a backup to enable data recovery in case of data loss

- As a source of data for forming replica files

---

[2] https://dev.mysql.com/doc/refman/5.6/en/backup-strategy-summary.html, MySQL

- As a source of data for experimentation: to create a copy of a database that you can use without editing the original data or to test potential upgrade incompatibilities

Depending on whether the --tab option is included or not, mysqldump produces two types of output:

- **Without --tab:** mysqldump issues SQL statements to the standard output. This output consists of CREATE statements to issue dumped objects such as databases, tables, and stored routines, and INSERT statements to load data into tables. The output can be placed in a file and reloaded later using MySQL to recreate the dumped objects. Options are available to modify the format of the SQL statements and to regulate which objects are dumped.

- **With --tab:** mysqldump produces two output files for each dumped table. The server provides one file as tab-delimited text, one line per table row. This file is named tbl_name.txt in the output directory. The server also sends a CREATE TABLE statement for the table to mysqldump, which writes it as a file named tbl_name.sql in the output directory.

By default, mysqldump saves the information as SQL statements to the standard output. You can save the output in a file similar to:[3]

```
shell> mysqldump [arguments] > file_name
```

---

[3] https://dev.mysql.com/doc/mysql-backup-excerpt/8.0/en/backup-types.html, MySQL

In order to dump all databases, add mysqldump with the
--all-databases option:

```
shell> mysqldump --all-databases > dump.sql
```

In order to dump only specific databases, insert the name
on the command line and use the --databases option:

```
shell> mysqldump --databases db1 db2 db3 >
dump.sql
```

The --databases option causes all names on the command
line to be referred to as database names. Without this
option, mysqldump registers the first name as a database
name and those following as table names.

With --all-databases or --databases, mysqldump
adds CREATE DATABASE and USE statements before
any dump output is produced for each database. This
ensures that when the dump file is reloaded, it creates each database if it does not exist and makes it the
default database so database contents are loaded into
the same database from which they came. If you need
to cause the dump file to force a drop of each database
before recreating it, apply the --add-drop-database
option as well. In this case, mysqldump writes a DROP
DATABASE statement that comes with each CREATE
DATABASE statement.

In order to dump a single database, name it on the command line:

```
shell> mysqldump --databases test > dump.
sql
```

In the single-database case, it is allowed to omit the --databases option:

```
shell> mysqldump test > dump.sql
```

The difference between the two preceding commands is that without --databases, the dump output contains no CREATE DATABASE or USE statements. This has several implications:

- If you reload the dump file, you should indicate a default database name so that the server knows which database to reload.

- When reloading, you can specify a database name different from the original name, which enables you to reload the data into a different database.

- If the database to be reloaded does not exist, you should create it first.

- Because the output holds no CREATE DATABASE statement, the --add-drop-database option has no effect. If you apply it, it produces no DROP DATABASE statement.

In order to dump only specific tables from a database, name them on the command line following the database name:

```
shell> mysqldump test t1 t3 t7 > dump.sql
```

If you call for mysqldump with the --tab=dir_name option, it uses dir_name as the output directory and dumps tables individually in that directory using two files for each table. The table name is the base name for these files. For a table named t1, the files are named t1.sql and t1.txt. The .sql file contains a CREATE TABLE statement for the table. The .txt file contains the table data, one line per table row.

The following command dumps the contents of the db1 database to files in the/tmp database:[4]

```
shell> mysqldump --tab=/tmp db1
```

The .txt files containing table data are scripted by the server, so they belong to the system account used for running the server. The server uses SELECT ... INTO OUTFILE to write the files, so you should have the FILE privilege to complete this operation, and an error occurs if a given .txt file already exists.

The server also sends the CREATE definitions for dumped tables to mysqldump, which writes them to .sql files. These files, therefore, belong to the user who executes mysqldump.

It is most suitable that --tab is used only for dumping a local server. If you apply it with a remote server, the --tab directory should exist on both the local and remote hosts, and the .txt files are written by the server in the remote directory (on the server host), while the .sql files are written by mysqldump in the local directory (on the client host).

For mysqldump --tab, the server by default scripts table data to .txt files one line per row with tabs between column values, no quotation marks around column values, and newline as the line terminator.

---

[4] https://dev.mysql.com/doc/mysql-backup-excerpt/8.0/en/mysqldump-delimited-text.html, MySQL

To enable data files to be written using a different format, mysqldump supports these options:[5]

- **fields-terminated-by=str:** The string applied for separating column values (default: tab)

- **fields-enclosed-by=char:** The character within which to locate column values (default: no character)

- **fields-optionally-enclosed-by=char:** The character within which to locate non-numeric column values (default: no character)

- **fields-escaped-by=char:** The character for escaping special characters (default: no escaping)

- **lines-terminated-by=str:** The line-termination string (default: newline)

Depending on the value you indicate for any of these options, it might be necessary on the command line to quote or escape the value according to your command interpreter. Alternatively, you can also specify the value using hex notation. For instance, you might want mysqldump to quote column values within double quotation marks. To do so, you can either specify double quote as the value for the --fields-enclosed-by option or specify the value in hex:

```
--fields-enclosed-by=0x22
```

---

[5] https://dev.mysql.com/doc/mysql-backup-excerpt/8.0/en/mysqldump-delimited-text.html, MySQL

It is also normal to use several of the data-formatting options in combination. For example, to dump tables in CSV format with lines terminated by carriage-return/new-line pairs (\r\n), insert this command (enter it on a single line):[6]

```
shell> mysqldump --tab=/tmp
--fields-terminated-by=,
        --fields-enclosed-by='"' --lines-
terminated-by=0x000a db1
```

In case you consider using any of the data-formatting options to dump table data, you must specify the same format when you reload data files later, to ensure correct interpretation of the file contents. In addition, there are several options that regulate how mysqldump handles stored programs:

```
--events: Dump Event Scheduler events
--routines: Dump stored procedures and
functions
--triggers: Dump triggers for tables
```

The --triggers option is activated by default so that when tables are dumped, they are accompanied by any triggers they have. The other options are disabled by default and should be specified to dump the corresponding objects. To disable any of these options explicitly, you can use its skip form: --skip-events, --skip-routines, or --skip-triggers.

---

[6] https://dev.mysql.com/doc/mysql-backup-excerpt/8.0/en/mysqldump-delimited-text.html, MySQL

## RESTORING FROM A BACKUP FILE

No one is 100% safe from experiencing a catastrophic unexpected exit that would require recovery from backups. In order to recover, you first need to restore the last full backup you have done (let's take the one from Friday 1 p.m. example). The full backup file is just a set of SQL statements, so restoring it is quite straightforward:

```
shell> MySQL < backup_tuesday_1_PM.sql
```

After that, the data will be restored to its state as of Friday 1 p.m. To restore the changes made since then, you should use the incremental backups; that is, the gbi-bin.000007 and gbi-bin.000008 binary log files. Transfer the files if necessary from where they were backed up, and then process their contents in the following format:

```
shell> mysqlbinlog gbi-bin.000007 gbi-bin.000008 | MySQL
```

Once that is fully processed, you would get access to the restored, but a few changes from that date to the date of the crash would still be missing. In order not to lose them, you would have to store all the MySQL binary logs into a safe location different from the place where it locates its data files, so that these logs were not on the damaged disk. So that you would be able to start the server with a --log-bin option that specifies a location on a different physical device from the one on which the data directory resides. That way, the logs are safe even if the device containing the directory is destroyed. If you had done this, you would have the gbi-bin.000009 file and any subsequent files available, and you could apply them using mysqlbinlog and MySQL to restore the most recent data changes with no loss up to the moment of the crash in the following way:

```
shell> mysqlbinlog gbi-bin.000009 … | mysql
```

To reload a dump file scripted by mysqldump that holds SQL statements, you can use it as input to the MySQL client. If the dump file was created by mysqldump with the --all-databases or --databases option, it has to CREATE DATABASE and USE statements and it is not necessary to specify a default database into which to load the data:

```
shell> MySQL < dump.sql
```

Alternatively, from within MySQL, you can use a source command:

```
mysql> source dump.sql
```

If the file is a single-database dump not containing CREATE DATABASE and USE statements, create the database first:

```
shell> mysqladmin create db1
```

And only after that specify the database name when you load the dump file:

```
shell> MySQL db1 < dump.sql
```

Alternatively, from within MySQL, create the database, select it as the default database, and load the dump file:

```
mysql> CREATE DATABASE IF NOT EXISTS db1;
mysql> USE db1;
mysql> source dump.sql
```

### Reloading Delimited-Text Format Backups

For backups activated with mysqldump --tab, each table is represented in the output directory by an .sql file containing the CREATE TABLE statement for the table, and a .txt file containing the table data. To reload a table, you would need to change its location into the output directory first. Then process the .sql file with MySQL to create an empty table and process the .txt file to load the data into the table:[7]

```
shell> mysql db1 < t1.sql
shell> mysqlimport db1 t1.txt
```

---

[7] https://dev.mysql.com/doc/mysql-backup-excerpt/8.0/en/reloading-delimited-text-dumps.html, MySQL

An alternative to using mysqlimport to load the data file is to insert the LOAD DATA statement from within the MySQL client:

```
mysql> USE db1;
mysql> LOAD DATA INFILE 't1.txt' INTO TABLE
t1;
```

In case you used any data-formatting options with mysql-dump when you initially dumped the table, you should use the same options with mysqlimport or LOAD DATA to ensure proper interpretation of the data file contents:

```
shell> mysqlimport --fields-terminated-by=,
        --fields-enclosed-by='"' --lines-
terminated-by=0x0d0a db1 t1.txt
Or:
mysql> USE db1;
mysql> LOAD DATA INFILE 't1.txt' INTO TABLE
t1
        FIELDS TERMINATED BY ',' FIELDS
ENCLOSED BY '"'
        LINES TERMINATED BY '\r\n';
```

This way, you can ensure the point-in-time recovery of data changes up to a given point in time. Normally, this type of recovery is done after restoring a full backup that brings the server to its state as of the time the backup was processed. Point-in-time recovery then regulated the server up to date incrementally from the time of the full backup to a more recent moment.

## Point-in-Time Recovery Using Binary Log

Many of the examples in this and previous chapters use the MySQL client to process binary log output created by mysqlbinlog. But in case your binary log contains\0 (null) characters, that output cannot be accepted by MySQL unless you insert it with the --binary-mode option.

The source of information for point-in-time recovery is the set of binary log files generated subsequent to the full backup operation. Therefore, to permit a server to be restored to a point-in-time, binary logging must be regulated for it.

In order to restore data from the binary log, you should know the name and location of the current binary log files. By default, the server produces binary log files in the data directory, but a pathname can be identified with the --log-bin option to locate the files in a different place. If you want to see a listing of all binary log files, you can use this statement:

```
mysql> SHOW BINARY LOGS;
```

In addition, to determine the name of the current binary log file, add the following statement:

```
mysql> SHOW MASTER STATUS;
```

The mysqlbinlog utility has the capacity to convert the events in the binary log files from binary format to text so that they can be further applied. mysqlbinlog has options for choosing sections of the binary log based on event times or position of events within the log.

Applying events from the binary log results in data modifications as well as recovery of data changes for a given span of time. To apply events from the binary log, process mysqlbinlog output with the MySQL client:

```
shell> mysqlbinlog binlog_files | mysql -u
root -p
```

Viewing log contents can be particularly handy when you need to decide on event times or positions to select partial log contents before implementing events. To view events from the log, add mysqlbinlog output into a paging program like this:

```
shell> mysqlbinlog binlog_files | more
```

Alternatively, copy the output in a file and view the file from a text editor:[8]

```
shell> mysqlbinlog binlog_files > tmpfile
shell> … edit tmpfile …
```

Copying the output in a file is useful as a preliminary to implementing the log contents with certain events deleted, such as an accidental DROP TABLE. You can remove from the file any statements not to be used before executing its contents. After modifying the file, apply the contents in the following format:

```
shell> MySQL -u root -p < tmpfile
```

---

[8] https://dev.mysql.com/doc/refman/5.6/en/point-in-time-recovery.html, MySQL

In case you have more than one binary log to use on the MySQL server, the safest option would be to process them all using a single connection to the server. To illustrate an example of how the unsafe option looks like:

```
shell> mysqlbinlog binlog.000001 | MySQL
-u root -p # DANGER!!
shell> mysqlbinlog binlog.000002 | MySQL
-u root -p # DANGER!!
```

Processing binary logs using different connections to the server might cause problems if the first log file has a CREATE TEMPORARY TABLE statement and the second log holds a statement that uses the temporary table. When the first MySQL process is completed, the server drops the temporary table. And if the second MySQL process tries to use the table, the server reports "unknown table."

To prevent difficulties as such from occurring, use a single connection to apply the contents of all binary log files that you want to process. The simplest way to do it:

```
shell> mysqlbinlog binlog.000001
binlog.000002 | MySQL -u root -p
```

Another method would include writing the whole log to a single file and then process the file:

```
shell> mysqlbinlog binlog.000001 > /tmp/
statements.sql
shell> mysqlbinlog binlog.000002 >> /tmp/
statements.sql
```

```
shell> mysql -u root -p -e "source/tmp/
statements.sql"
```

When writing to a dump file while reading back from a binary log containing Global Transaction Identifiers (GTID), insert the --skip-gtids option with mysqlbinlog, in this manner:[9]

```
shell> mysqlbinlog --skip-gtids
binlog.000001 > /tmp/dump.sql
shell> mysqlbinlog --skip-gtids
binlog.000002 >> /tmp/dump.sql
shell> mysql -u root -p -e "source/tmp/
dump.sql"
```

Now let's review the operation in detail using an example. As an illustration, imagine that around 13:00:00 on May 25, 2021, an SQL statement was activated that removed a table. Therefore, you should complete a point-in-time recovery to restore the server up to its condition right before the table deletion. Fundamental steps to achieve that include the following:

Firstly, restore the last full backup created before the point-in-time of interest. When done, note the binary log position up to which you have restored the server for later use, and restart the server.

At this point, your backup and restore tool should be able to provide you with the last binary log position for your recovery. For instance, if you are using mysqlbinlog for the task, check the stop position of the binary log replay; or in case you are using MySQL Enterprise Backup, the last binary log position has been saved in your backup.

---

[9] https://dev.mysql.com/doc/refman/5.6/en/point-in-time-recovery.html, MySQL

The next step would be to find the exact binary log event position referring to the point in time up to which you need to restore your database. In addition, if you know the rough time where the table deletion took place, you can find the log position by checking the log contents around that time using the mysqlbinlog utility. Make sure to apply the --start-Date-Time and --stop-datetime options to identify a short time period around the event, and then look for it in the output.

After that, apply the events in binary log file to the server, starting with the log position you found in step 1 (assume it is 1006) and ending at the position you have found in step 2 that is before your point-in-time of interest (which is 1868):[10]

```
shell> mysqlbinlog --start-position=1006
--stop-position=1868 /var/lib/mysql/
bin.123456 \
          | mysql -u root -p
```

This command would recover all the transactions from the starting position until just before the stop position. And since the output of mysqlbinlog includes SET TIMESTAMP statements before each SQL statement recorded, the recovered data and related MySQL logs would reflect the original times at which the transactions were implemented. With these, your database would by now be restored to the point-in-time of interest, right before any charges were dropped.

Additionally, in case you also need to execute all the statements after your point-in-time of interest, use mysql-binlog again to apply all the events to the server. So, after the statement we wanted to skip, the log is at position 1985;

---

[10] https://dev.mysql.com/doc/refman/5.6/en/point-in-time-recovery.html, MySQL

thus, we can use it for the --start-position option, so that any statements after the position are included:

```
shell> mysqlbinlog --start-position=1985 /
var/lib/MySQL/bin.123456 \
        | MySQL -u root -p
```

With that command, your database has been restored the latest statement recorded in the binary log file, but with the selected event skipped.

## DUMPING DATA IN CSV FORMAT

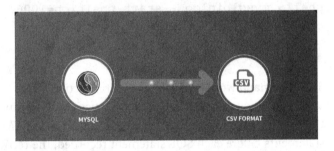

A comma-separated values (CSV) file is a standard format that has a number of great benefits:

- It is a widely accepted format.

- CSV files have the great advantage of being readable by users.

- Being plain-text, they can easily be transferred into any application.

- Mostly used to organize large databases.

In this section, we shall look through five methods to export your tables from MySQL to CSV via: using the command line, through mysqldump, MySQL Workbench, phpMyAdmin, or by using the CSV engine.

1. **Using Command Line:** It is extremely simple to add the command line to export a MySQL table to CSV. There is no need to download any additional software. All you have to do is follow the guideline on exporting to CSV using the command line under the following conditions: exporting selected columns of a table, exporting tables with a timestamp, tables with Column Headers, and learn how to handle NULL Values.

   **Step 1:** Navigate to the database which has the table you need to export by inserting the following command: USE dbName

   Here, dbName must be replaced with the name of your database. If your MySQL server has been started with –secure-file-priv option, you should use:

   ```
   SHOW VARIABLES LIKE "secure_file_priv"
   ```

   This command will display the directory that has been configured so that you can later store your output file in this directory.

   **Step 2:** After that, select all the data of the table and identify the location of the output file in the following format:[11]

---

[11] https://hevodata.com/learn/mysql-export-to-csv/, Hevo Data

```
TABLE tableName
INTO OUTFILE 'path/outputFile.csv'
FIELDS TERMINATED BY ','
OPTIONALLY ENCLOSED BY '"'
ESCAPED BY "
LINES TERMINATED BY 'n';
```

Here, make sure to add the .csv extension for your output file. The ORDER clause can be applied to organize the data according to a specific attribute. The LIMIT clause is used to regulate the number of rows to be placed into the output file.

a. **Exporting Selected Columns of a Table:** In order to export selected columns of a table, you can use the SELECT statement to specify the columns you want to export. It is also possible to apply the WHERE clause to use specific conditions and filter the results:

```
SELECT columnName, …
FROM tableName
WHERE columnName = 'value';
```

b. **Exporting Tables with a Timestamp:** At times you might need to add a timestamp to the exported file and to do that you should use a MySQL prepared statement. Insert the following command to export to a CSV file, and add a timestamp for the time the file was created:[12]

---

[12] https://hevodata.com/learn/mysql-export-to-csv/, Hevo Data

```
SET @TS = DATE_FORMAT(NOW(),'_%Y_%m_
%d_%H_%i_%s');
SET @FOLDER = '/var/lib/sql-files/';
SET @PREFIX = 'employees';
SET @EXT = '.csv';
SET @CMD = CONCAT("SELECT * FROM
tableName INTO OUTFILE '",@FOLDER,@
PREFIX,@TS,@EXT,
"'FIELDS ENCLOSED BY '"
'TERMINATED BY ','
ESCAPED BY '"'",
"LINES TERMINATED BY 'n';");
PREPARE statement FROM @CMD;
EXECUTE statement;
```

c. **Export with Column Headers:** It is often easier just to add column headers to the output file to better review the data. To complete this, you should use the UNION statement. Insert the following command to add column headers:

```
(SELECT 'columnHeading', …)
UNION
(SELECT column, …
FROM tableName
INTO OUTFILE 'path-to-file/
outputFile.csv''
FIELDS ENCLOSED BY '"'
TERMINATED BY ','
ESCAPED BY '"'
LINES TERMINATED BY 'n')
```

d. **Handling NULL Values:** If your output has NULL values, they will be displayed as 'N' in the exported file instead of NULL. This may result in confusion and to prevent that, you may want to replace this 'N' string with a string like NA (not applicable) that is more comprehensible. Insert the following command to do it:

```
SELECT column, column,
IFNULL(column, 'NA')
FROM tableName INTO OUTFILE 'path-
to-file/outputFile.csv'
FIELDS ENCLOSED BY '"'
TERMINATED BY ','
ESCAPED BY '"'
LINES TERMINATED BY 'n');
```

2. **Using mysqldump:** mysqldump is a great tool provided by MySQL server that lets users export tables, databases and entire servers. Furthermore, it is also used for backup and recovery. All you have to do is just use the following command in a command prompt/terminal:

```
mysqldump -u [username] -p -t -T/path/
to/directory [database] [tableName]
--fields-terminated-by=,
```

The added command will produce a copy of the table specified by tableName at the location you choose using the -T option. The name of the file will be similar to that of the table and will have a .txt extension.

3. **Using MySQL Workbench:** MySQL Workbench has an Import/Export Wizard that allows you to export database/tables to a specified format using a graphical user interface. The wizard also supports JSON and CSV formats. You can follow this order to export your MySQL table using MySQL Workbench:

**Step 1:** Use the left bar "schemas" tab to choose the table you want to export.

**Step 2:** Right-click on the table and select "Table Data Export Wizard." Next, choose the columns you want to export.

**Step 3:** Click on Next to be able to see the directory where you want to save the output file. There make sure to choose the CSV format option.

**Step 4:** Click on Next, and your data will start exporting. You will be able to track the process through the logs.

4. **Using phpMyAdmin:** phpMyAdmin has a graphical user interface to export your MySQL table in different formats. Apart from CSV, it supports other formats such as XML, JSON, and YAML. In order to use phpMyAdmin to export data, follow these steps:

**Step 1:** Log in to phpMyAdmin using a user that has required permissions and Navigate to the database which contains the source table.

**Step 2:** Choose the table from the database and then click on Export in the top bar.

**Step 3:** Select the CSV format from the Format drop-down menu and click on Go. Make sure to select Save file option when prompted.

5. **Using CSV Engine:** The CSV storage engine locates data in text files using CSV format and at most time compiles it into the MySQL server. It is important to remember that this method can only be used if the table does not have an index or an AUTO_ INCREMENT limitations.

ALTER TABLE tableName ENGINE=CSV command changes the format of the database to CSV so that it can then be easily copied to another system.

With these five methods to export your MySQL table to CSV, you should by now be comfortable with writing queries using the command-line or mysql-dump utility tool. Nevertheless, if you are still not fully confident with your querying skills, MySQL Workbench and phpMyAdmin will be the simplest way to complete the task.

## TRANSFERRING DATA FROM ONE MySQL SERVER TO ANOTHER

Transferring or Migrating a MySQL database between servers normally takes only a few easy steps but depending on the volume of data you would like to transfer, it might take some time. We recommend checking a few points to ensure a smooth procedure before transferring:

- Make sure to have the same version of MySQL installed on both servers with the same distribution.

- Make sure to have enough free space on both servers to accommodate the database dump file and the imported database.

- It is not advised to move the data directory of the database to another server. The internal structure of the database should not be involved in this process.

There might be many instances when you would require to migrate the MySQL database between two servers, like cloning a database for testing, a separate database for collecting reports, or completely migrating the database system to a new server. Based on a standard approach, you will need to take a backup of data on the first server, transfer it remotely to the destination server and then restore the backup on the new MySQL instance. Step by step process looks like this:

**Step 1:** Backup the Data

**Step 2:** Copying the Database Dump on the Destination Server

**Step 3:** Restoring the Dump

1. **Backup the Data:** The first step to transfer MySQL database is to take a dump of the data that you want to move. In order to do that, you will have to use the mysqldump command. The basic syntax of the command is: mysqldump -u [username] -p [database] > dump.sql

   In case the database is on a remote server, either log in to that system using ssh or use -h and -P options to provide host and port respectively:

```
mysqldump -P [port] -h [host] -u
[username] -p [database] > dump.sql
```

In addition, there are also various special options available for this command:

```
mysqldump -u [username] -p [database]
> dump.sql - this command dumps
specified database to the file.
```

You can specify multiple databases for the dump using the following command:

```
mysqldump -u [username] -p --databases
[database1] [database2] > dump.sql
```

Or you can also use –all-databases option to backup all databases on the MySQL instance:

```
mysqldump -u [username] -p --all-
databases > dump.sql
```

Above mentioned commands dump all the tables in the specified database, but in case you need to take backup of some specific tables, you can use the following command:

```
mysqldump -u [username] -p [database]
[table1] [table2] > dump.sql
```

It is also possible to backup data using some custom query, for that you will need to use the following WHERE option provided by mysqldump:

```
mysqldump -u [username] -p [database]
[table1] --where="WHERE CLAUSE" > dump.
sql
```

By default, mysqldump command includes DROP TABLE and CREATE TABLE statements in the created dump. Therefore, if you are using incremental backups or you specifically requested to restore data without deleting previous data, make sure you use the –no-create-info option while creating a dump:

```
mysqldump -u [username] -p [database]
--no-create-info > dump.sql
```

When you need to just copy the schema but not the data, you can use –no-data option while creating the dump:

```
mysqldump -u [username] -p [database]
--no-data > dump.sql
```

2. **Copying the Database Dump on the Destination Server:** Once you have created the dump as per your specification, the next step would be to transfer the data dump file to the destination server. You will have to use Scp command for that:

```
Scp -P [port] [dump_file].sql
[username]@[servername]:[path on
destination]
```

3. **Restoring the Dump:** The last step is restoring the data on the destination server. MySQL command directly provides a way to restore to dump data to the MySQL:

```
MySQL -u [username] -p [database] <
[dump_file].sql
```

To sum up, if you follow the steps mentioned above, you can quickly transfer your database between two servers, but it might get slightly tiresome if it turns to be a recurring task. It is common for middle-sized or bigger companies to hire a separate database manager who would only take care of such unction and manage all the data pipelines in a fault-free manner.

# Appraisal

Let's face it—we deal with databases every day. What do you do when you want to listen to your favorite songs? You open your playlist from your smartphone, and in this case, you are accessing the playlist database. When you take a selfie and upload it to your profile on a social network platform, your photo gallery performs as a database. When you browse any e-commerce website to buy clothes, you refer to the shopping cart as a database. Clearly, databases are everywhere. And merely by definition, a database stands for a structured collection of data.

A database that regulates the data relating to each other by nature or an item to a particular product category and associates it with multiple tags is called a relational database. In the relational database, we model data like products, categories, and tags by using tables. A table contains columns and rows that look like a spreadsheet. MySQL in this case, is a unique open-source database management system that allows you to operate relational databases.

The basic plan of the client-server structure has the following format: One or more devices (clients) connect to a server through a specific network. Every client can make a request from the graphical user interface (GUI) on their screens, and the server will put together the desired output, as long as both ends understand the instruction. Without getting too technical, the main processes taking place in a MySQL environment described in Chapter 3:

- In the beginning, MySQL creates a database for storing and manipulating data, explicitly determining the relationship of each table.

- Clients then can make requests by typing specific SQL statements on MySQL.

- The server application has to respond with the requested information that appears on the clients' side.

That is pretty much it. From the clients' side, they usually emphasize which MySQL GUI to use. The lighter and more user-friendly the GUI is, the faster and easier their data management activities will be. Some of the most popular MySQL GUIs are MySQL WorkBench, SequelPro, DBVisualizer, and the Navicat DB Admin Tool. Some are free, while some are commercial, some run exclusively for macOS, and some are compatible with major operating systems. You should be able to choose the GUI depending on your needs and requirements.

To make it clear, MySQL is not the only relative database on the market, but it is considered to be one of the most popular ones scoring great points at critical parameters like the number of downloads, mentions in search results, and frequency of technical discussions on Internet forums. In addition, the fact that many major tech giants rely on it further verifies the well-deserved reputation. Here are a few reasons why people trust it:

1. **Data Security:** It is globally renowned for being one of the most secure and reliable database management systems used in popular web applications like WordPress, Drupal, Joomla, Facebook, and Twitter. The data security and support for transactional processing that comes with the recent version of MySQL can significantly benefit any enterprise, especially if it is an eCommerce business that involves frequent financial transactions.

2. **On-Demand Scalability:** MySQL can offer almost unmatched scalability to facilitate the management of deeply embedded apps using a smaller footprint even in massive warehouses that store terabytes of data. On-demand flexibility is another popular feature of MySQL. This open-source solution can efficiently complete the customization of any eCommerce business with unique database server requirements.

3. **High Performance:** MySQL has an impressive storage-engine framework that facilitates system administrators to adjust the MySQL database server for better performance. Whether it is an eCommerce website that processes a million queries every single day or a high-speed transactional processing system, MySQL is made to meet even the most demanding requests while ensuring optimum speed, full-text indexes, and great memory caches for professional performance.

4. **Round-The-Clock Uptime:** MySQL comes with the benefit of 24/7 uptime and has a wide range of high availability solutions like specialized cluster servers and replication modifications.

5. **Comprehensive Transactional Support:** MySQL is definitely on the top list of robust transactional database solutions available on the market. With attributes like complete atomic, consistent, isolated, durable transaction support, multi-version transaction support, and unrestricted row-level locking, it is the ideal solution for complete data integrity. It can also guarantee instant deadlock identification through server-enforced referential integrity.

6. **Complete Workflow Control:** With the typical download and installation time being less than 30 minutes, MySQL ensures great usability from day one. Whether your platform is Linux, Microsoft, Macintosh, or UNIX, MySQL is a suitable solution with self-management characteristics that automate most activities from space configuration to data design and database modeling.

7. **Reduced Total Cost of Ownership:** By transferring current database applications to MySQL, enterprises can enjoy significant cost savings on their projects. The dependability and ease of management that come with MySQL save your problem-solving time which is otherwise wasted in preventing downtime issues and operational problems.

8. **The Flexibility of Open Source:** It is often that users worry about the installation and maintenance of any open source solutions. However, My SQL's round-the-clock support and enterprise indemnification can definitely put an end to it. The secure processing and trusted software of MySQL altogether can provide effective transactions for large volume activities. It ensures error-free maintenance, debugging, and upgrades in order to enhance the end-user experience.

At the same time, the bigger the scope of data circulates in an organization, the more advanced data modeling tool is required. Data modeling was defined as a process of operating and analyzing data models for resources located in a database. It could be treated as an abstract system that regulates the data specification, data semantic, and consistency limitations of data. Its main aim is to manage data types within a structure, the relationships between objects, and their characteristics. The data model could help you to realize what data is necessary and how it should be arranged properly. It is like a guideline for a professional to better set and catalog what is being produced.

The functionality potential of MySQL in terms of data modeling can be broad and quite impressive. The main features of the database in relation to data modeling are the following: compatibility with various models, capacity to produce new models, support for common modeling activities, and management of relationships and dependencies between models and their items.

It is also important to keep in mind that creating and overseeing a data model would require collaboration among different management areas (data architect, business stakeholders, product-users). The use of data modeling software connects and sets the information flow as well as verifies the correct representation of all data items. Additionally, it helps when searching for missing and redundant data. The end result of the above advantages is a reduction of very time-consuming data modeling activities and consequently saving resources for the organization.

Similarly, with MySQL, there is no need to keep re-issuing the individual statements every time they are requested. They can simply refer to the stored routine instead. A stored routine could be defined as a named package of SQL statements located on the server. We have reviewed two main stored routine types:

- **Stored procedures:** Ones that invoke procedures with a CALL statement. They can pass back values using output variables or result sets.

- **Stored functions:** Also referred to as call functions inside a statement that return scalar values.

Apart from that, one of the main activities typically performed by developers is to manage SQL scripts and environments for the database. While managing multiple copies, sometimes it requires refreshing from a production environment to a lower environment. For that you are expected to copy all database objects such as database schema, tables, as well as use multiple approaches such as database backup restore, depending upon the requirement.

MySQL uses Generate Scripts wizard to script all database objects or specific objects. It provides various configuration options to select from. You should start by right-clicking on the source SQL database for which you want to generate script and launch Generate scripts wizard that comes with a brief introduction and activity options to choose from: Select database objects, Specify scripting options, Generate scripts and save them, or Generate Scripts Wizard for database objects.

And as the number of users and database entities increases, user management and security control are two areas that quickly become multiplex. Managing many different privileges on different database objects, making sure users have the same level of responsibilities access, monitoring, and inspecting access can become more difficult with time. To help with this, MySQL came up with a concept called "roles" that allows you to group sets of privileges under a given name, letting you assign and edit overarching settings. Like user accounts, you can grant privileges to roles and revoke privileges from them. If you want to grant the same set of privileges to multiple users, you need to create a new role, grant privileges to the role, and then grant the role to the users. When you need to change the privileges of the users, you should change the privileges of the granted role only. The changes will take effect to all users to which the role is granted.

It is a fact that your network applications almost entirely depend upon databases. Most of what you work with typically depends upon a database or two. Because of that, it is highly recommended to have backups of those databases and learn how to export and import them from either machine or database server. Importing and exporting databases should not be feared but instead considered as a regular task in software development. You can use data dumps to back up and migrate data to a new server or development environment.

In Chapter 6, we learned how to work with database dumps in MySQL and establish a step-by-step approach on how to export a database and then import that same database from the dump file. In addition, we have found out how to transfer or migrate a MySQL database between servers.

Backup and restoration of MySQL databases play a key role in a production environment. It is important to back up your databases so that you can recover your data and be up and running again in case issues like hardware crashes, system failures occur. Backups are also essential as a safeguard before upgrading a MySQL installation, and they can be utilized to transfer a MySQL installation to another system or to organize replica servers. We have been able to focus on the most common tools for generating backups in several formats as well as see what types and characteristics are there. To sum up, we have looked at what raw files Physical and Logical Backups consist of, research about the difference between Online and Offline Backups, Local and Remote Backups, Snapshot Backups, Full and Incremental Backups.

However, most open-source tools, including MySQL, are now facing particular development challenges that happen when you do not consider thoroughly what is needed from a data stack to maintain consistent service and powerful analytics. Several points for further MySQL improvement should include the following:

1. There is a need to increase data storage and compute strains on the system. This request typically comes from larger customers. Now open source solutions still require manual and disruptive scaling that impacts the customer experience and requires more time and effort for engineering.

2. Users observe a lack of native support for semi-structured data as using data types such as JSON, XML, and Avro is a huge challenge, especially when the open-source solution does not natively support semi-structured data. This forces experts to set and maintain complex data pipelines.

3. While development teams should spend their time coding and developing analytics applications, open-source solutions also require frequent upgrades and maintenance. As a result, developers end up spending most of their time and resources dealing with system maintenance instead of what they are supposed to do in the first place—coding.

4. The use of open-source tools mostly requires specific skills that may not exist within an organization. Consequently, companies need to hire more experts, which is typically problematic to find and expensive to attain.

With these ongoing discussions in mind, the SQL Server development tools have to rush and streamline the application development process. At the same time, we know that the SQL Server development applications have a rich integrated development environment, able to provide an opportunity for object re-use, integrate with source control applications like Visual Source Safe, and great potential to re-establish itself in response to new challenges.

# Index